S0-DRZ-491

MAIMONIDES

BY THE SAME AUTHOR

Megillat Taanit as a Source for Jewish Chronology and History in the Hellenistic and Roman Periods.
Out of print

Studies in Beginnings of Christianity.
Out of print

Josephus on Jesus with Particular Reference to the Slavonic Josephus and the Hebrew Josippon.
Price, $2.00

An Historical Study of the Canonization of the Hebrew Scriptures. *Price, $0.60*

The History of the Second Jewish Commonwealth Prolegomena. *Price, $1.50*

MOSES MAIMONIDES

MAIMONIDES

A BIOGRAPHY

BY

SOLOMON ZEITLIN, Ph.D.

NEW YORK

BLOCH PUBLISHING CO.

"The Jewish Book Concern"

1935

Copyright, 1935
by
SOLOMON ZEITLIN

TO

MY PARENTS

PREFACE

UNDOUBTEDLY Maimonides was the greatest scholar the Jews produced since the completion of the Talmud. There is no one who has had such profound influence upon Jewish life as he. Again, no Hebrew scholar has aroused such controversy which actually divided the Jewish people into two hostile camps.

Strange as it may seem, there is no complete biography of this Jewish genius. Many books have appeared dealing with his literary activity, particularly with his philosophy. Many articles, likewise, are to be found about his works in the various scholarly journals, both Jewish and non-Jewish. These however, deal with different phases of his life and works. A book of merit was published in 1908 by the *Gesellschaft zur Forderung der Wissenschaft des Judentums*, entitled *Moses ben Maimon* in which are found essays on his life, works and influence. In 1903 a biography of Maimonides, written by Israel Abrahams and David Yellin, was issued by the Jewish Publication Society. In 1912 there appeared another biography in German entitled *Moses ben Maimon* written by Münz. At present these two volumes are antiquated. The first one was published thirty-two years ago, and the latter twenty-three years ago. Since then, new material has come to light. Many Responsa which were previously unknown,

between the two opposing parties. Similarly, in order to understand the man perfectly a complete picture of the political and social conditions prevailing in Egypt is given.

I wish to express my indebtedness to my friend, Albert Mordell, for his devoted service to me, and to both him and my friend, Dr. Mortimer J. Cohen for their assistance and their readiness to help me in bringing this book to this form, and for their valuable suggestions for improvement in literary style. I also desire to express my gratitude to Dr. and Mrs. Cyrus Adler for reading the manuscript and for making helpful suggestions. I wish to express my appreciation to Dr. Sidney B. Hoenig for compiling the index and reading the proofs. I am very thankful to the Librarians and the Staff of Dropsie College and the Jewish Theological Seminary for placing at my disposal all the necessary books.

SOLOMON ZEITLIN.

March, 1935

CONTENTS

mendously impressed as well as astonished, for they had considered him a boy without any capacity for study.[3]

In 1148, a great catastrophe befell the Jewish community of Cordova. A few years earlier the Almohades (the Puritans), a fanatic sect of Islam, who were under the leadership of the Mahdi ibn Tumart and later under his successor Abd-el-mumin, conquered Morocco. This sect did not tolerate any other religion besides their own in the countries they ruled. Jews and Christians alike had to choose between Islam or exile. The Almohades crossed Gibraltar in 1148 and captured the city of Cordova. They destroyed synagogues and churches, and applied their policy of intolerance to the inhabitants of Cordova as they had done to those of Fez, compelling them to choose Islam or to leave the country. Those who did not emigrate but continued to live as Jews were unmercifully persecuted.

A vivid description of the persecution which befell the Jews at that time is given by a contemporary chronicler, Abraham ibn David (Rabad). In his *Sefer ha-Kabbalah* he writes as follows: "After the death of R. Joseph ha-Levi, the study of the Torah was interrupted, although he left a son and a nephew, both of whom had under his tuition become profound scholars. The righteous man (R. Joseph) was taken away on account of the approaching evils. After the death of R. Joseph there came for the Jews a time of oppression and distress. They abandoned their homes, 'Such as were for death, to death, and such as were for the sword, to the sword; and such as were for the famine, to the famine, and such as were for the captivity, to the captivity,' Jeremiah (xv. 2); and, paraphrasing Jeremiah, it might be added; 'such as were for apostasy, to apostasy.' All this was brought about by the sword of ibn Tumart, who in 4902 (1142), determined to blot out the name of Israel, and actually leave no trace of the Jews in any part of his empire."[4]

Many Jews fled with their belongings from Andalusia, some going to the northern part of Spain, which was a Christian country, others migrating to Provençal, France. Among the emigrants who left for northern Spain, was the family of Kimhi.[5] Nevetheless, a number of Jews remained in the country. Some of them accepted the religion of Mohammed openly, but secretly continued to live as Jews and observe the Jewish precepts. Others, however, did not declare themselves as Moslems, but disguised themselves in the dress of the natives so as not to be conspicuous as Jews. Among these were Maimon and his family. It was not difficult for them to use this disguise as Arabs, for the turbans they wore were similar to the Mohammedan head-gear, and they spoke Arabic perfectly. Continually exposed to the danger of detection, they could not stay in one city any length of time, and therefore they travelled from place to place.

The education of the lad, Moses, nevertheless, was not neglected by his father. In this period, when no Jewish schools, Yeshivot (places of learning) or synagogues existed, Moses continued his Jewish studies and occupied himself in research work. He pursued his secular studies, particularly philosophy, with great success.

He studied philosophy with the pupils of the famous philosopher, Abu Bekr ibn Alzaig and was also friendly with the son of ibn Aflah of Seville.[6] Already at this time he compiled commentaries on a few tractates of the Talmud.[7] He also wrote an essay on the Jewish calendar[8] and a short treatise on logical terms, *Millot Higgayon.*[9] Such youthful authorship showed that Moses ben Maimon, still in his early twenties, was a mature scholar, not only in Talmudic law but in mathematics and Aristotelian philosophy as well. He also displayed an effective and remarkably lucid style.

In 1158, when he was twenty-three years of age,[10] he began to write his well-known commentary on the Mishna in the Arabic language but used Hebrew characters. He gave it the title "Saraj" which in Hebrew is "Maor," Luminary. In the following year, Maimun and his family left Spain for Morocco.

II

IN MOROCCO

THE question now arises, why did Maimun and his family leave for Fez, Morocco? The Almohades who persecuted Jews as well as Christians in Spain, and destroyed synagogues as well churches, were the masters of Morocco and exhibited there the same spirit of intolerance and persecution. Judaism and Christianity were under a ban. One does not deliberately flee from persecution to a place where there is greater persecution. This migration of Maimon and his family to Morocco has led many scholars to believe that they had officially accepted the Mohammedan religion and considered themselves Moslems. They were classified as *Anusim*; proselytes, (force majeure).[1] This theory has been strengthened by the fact that an Arab, Abul Arab ibn Moisha, after Maimonides had settled in Egypt and occupied a high position there, informed the authorities that he had been a Moslem while in Morocco. Others, however, deny that Maimonides accepted the religion of Islam. They point out that at no time could he have been a Moslem; for never did his opponents, even in the heat of the controversies against him, accuse him of being an apostate.[2]

However, both of these theories are untenable. The elder Maimun never officially accepted Islam; he and his family simply disguised themselves as Arabs and thus deceived the authorities and avoided persecution. They tried to remain at home where they could observe the Law. They mingled very little with the people in order not to attract too much attention.

Maimonides, in his "*Iggeret ha Schemad*," Epistle on Apostasy, gives us a hint at the course of conduct pursued by his father, himself and the rest of the family. He says that this apostasy was an extraordinary one; for the Moslems demanded that the Jews only openly profess to believe in Mohammedanism, being perfectly aware that inwardly the Jews did not believe in it.

Even the most bigoted rabbis could never accuse Maimonides of being an apostate. Since he never actually accepted Mohammedanism but only disguised himself to resemble the Moslems, his conduct could not be considered a transgression against Jewish law.

It was a common occurrence for Jews to disguise themselves in the time of persecution. In Germany for example during the period of the Crusades, many Jews adopted disguises to save themselves from persecution by wearing the garments of the Christians. Some went so far as to wear a cross as a means of protection. Even Rabbi Judah, who in his book *Sefer Hasidim*, prohibited the Jews from wearing a cross to save their lives, permitted them to disguise themselves when necessary in dress.[3] He also permitted women who were in danger of being criminally attacked, to clothe themselves in the habiliments of men.[4]

On the other hand, the devotees of the Islamic religion never demanded external signs to show adherence to their faith. The charge of Abul Arab ibn Moisha that Maimonides had been a Moslem was apparently based on his recollections of Maimonides in Mohammedan dress.

This interpretation solves the problem why the opponents of Maimonides never tried to defame him by accusing him of having become a convert. Even were we to assume for argument's sake that he had at one time been a Moslem, still there is no doubt that the rabbis were compelled to remain silent on such a matter, for Rabbenu Gershom, the *Maor Hagolah* (The Luminary of the Exile), had declared a ban upon any Jew who would ever remark that a fellow Jew had at one time been a proselyte.[5]

It is very probable that the family of Maimun left Spain for Fez for the purpose of aiding Moses, who was then engaged in writing his commentary on the Mishna. He did not have the necessary books in Cordova nor were any distinguished rabbis there. Knowing that Rabbi Judah ibn Shoshan, the eminent scholar, was in Fez and that some Jewish activity was going on there underground, Maimun, and his two sons, Moses and David, left for Morocco.[6] Although the Almohades destroyed the synagogues and the churches they interfered little with secular activities. Schools of learning were still in existence in Morocco and were conducted by many scholars proficient in mathematics and medicine. Thus, Maimonides' thirst for knowledge, both Talmudic and secular, prompted the family to undertake this adventurous trip.

Upon their arrival in Morocco, they found the Jewish community in a deplorable state. Judaism was suppressed, and anyone who dared to observe the Jewish religion was put to death. The persecution of the Jews had already lasted more than a decade, causing many of them to become skeptical and to wonder whether Judaism was the true religion, and whether Islam had not superseded it. They even thought it possible that Mohammed was the true prophet who had come to replace Moses.

At that time there was a group of émigrés who succeeded in escaping from Morocco. Since they were thus no longer exposed to any danger in practising their Judaism, they denounced their co-religionists of Morocco by saying that they were not good Jews who for the sake of saving their lives even officially accepted Islam. The prayers of these *Anusim* would find no acceptance before God, they held, and it was futile for them to continue following the Jewish precepts secretly. Furthermore, the émigrés declared that anyone who accepted a human being as a prophet, even under compulsion, was to be considered a heathen, though he fulfill the entire Torah. An epistle expressing this opinion was written by a rabbi who had escaped from Morocco to a foreign country.

Thus, in consequence, both the expedient compliance

and the forced conversion prevailing among the Jews of Morocco were dangerous to the community for they might result in the extinction of Judaism. On the one hand, the Jews who yielded only lip service to Mohammed in order to save their lives were ready to give up Judaism entirely and turn to Islam wholeheartedly. On the other hand, the Jews who were forced to accept Islam and who continued to observe all the Jewish precepts at home exposed themselves thereby to the dangers of death and torture. These people were denounced by other Jews abroad as heretics. Their prayers to God, it was maintained, would not be accepted, since they were not true Jews.

Maimun, upon his arrival in Fez, in 1160, realizing the dangers of the situation, composed in Arabic a letter of consolation filled with religious sentiment to his brethren in Morocco.[7] He persisted in his faith that Israel was still the beloved son of God. God could not despise those whom He once chose. He did not favor some one and then in fickleness reject him. His promises should no more be doubted than His existence. Although the Jews were suffering now while their oppressors were powerful, it must not be believed that He had forsaken His people. It was the duty of the Jew to return unto Him, He would certainly not abandon Israel; he had promised this to Moses. The precepts should be observed as much as possible in time of persecution but without incurring danger. It was particularly important that prayers should not cease. If they could not be offered at set times, they should be said silently, and God would certainly accept them with mercy.

Maimonides, emulating his father, also wrote a letter, addressing it to that group of Jews which had been denounced by their co-religionists for having accepted Islam. Their detractors, it will be recalled, had declared that although these Jews secretly observed the Jewish religion they were now without hope and were no longer considered as Jews. This letter, written in Arabic, was called *Maamar Kiddush Hashem*—a Treatise on the Sanctification of God—better known as *Iggeretha-Schemad*—Letter on Apostasy. In this letter, Maimonides bitterly opposed the opinion of the fanatics in reference to the *Anusim*. He held that such an opinion was not only unjust to the *Anusim*, but was a gross misrepresentation of Judaism. He proved from Talmudic passages that it was not considered a sin for anyone to disguise himself in a time of religious persecution in order to save his life. He appealed to precedent in the time of the persecution by the Romans. Rabbis Meir and Eliezar had saved their lives by pretending that they were not Jews.[8] Maimonides argued passionately: Would these fanatics consider Rabbi Meir a non-Jew? How could one unjustly designate as heathens Jews forced to accept Islam who continued secretly to observe the Jewish law? Rabbi Meir acted like them and yet did not lose his rabbinic authority. Maimonides also repudiated the contention of the fanatics who maintained that if one entered a mosque, without praying there and later went home and prayed to God, he would not find his prayers answered. Maimonides presented by contrast the lenient observation of the Talmud upon the case of Ahab, King of Israel, who had denied God and worshipped idols, but afterwards fasted two hours and a half and prayed to God.[9] The Talmud said that his prayers were accepted and that God had mercy upon him.

Maimonides cited other instances in Jewish history, to show that even idol worshippers had been rewarded when they prayed to God. Beyond question, then, the Jews of Morocco who had been forced into apostasy but who had continued to practice Judaism would be rewarded by God. "Are these fanatics who expressed such an opinion," he asks, "healthy or mentally sick?"

He differentiated this forced apostasy from other apostasies in the past, where Jews had been compelled to transgress the Jewish law. In this apostasy, however, no overt act was required on their part. Only conformity in speech was required and the Moslems themselves knew that the Jews did not thereby really accept the Mohammedan religion. The Jews were not to be condemned when their compliance was for the purpose of being saved from persecution. Whoever was put to death because he would not accept Mohammed as the true prophet should be commended for his martyrdom. His reward was great before God. But if one were to inquire, "Shall I be slain or utter the formula?" the answer should be, "Utter the formula and live." His advice to one in such a dilemma was not to remain for any length of time in the country, and meanwhile to shut himself up in his own house as much as possible and secretly observe the precepts of God.

He had no patience with people who consoled themselves with the thought that the King Messiah would soon appear in the western countries and lead them to Jerusalem. They who remained in the country, anticipating the Messiah, were causing others to transgress the Law. Besides, there was no definite time when the Messiah would appear. It was not known whether his coming would be in the near future or at some remote period. A sincere wish to observe the Jewish law had no relation to the appearance of the Messiah. If God would grant the Jews the privilege of witnessing that great event it would be well. If not, the Jews should not lose faith but should continue in the observance of the Jewish tradition. The person who refused to be faithful to his religion and thought that he would remain in the country until the Messiah appeared was wasting his time. He was wicked, and practiced a course that ultimately led to the nullification of reason and religion.

To sum up Maimonides' views on this entire matter: He was of the opinion that one who desires to be faithful to his religion ought to leave the country where he is persecuted and go to a place where the Jewish religion is tolerated. There he may continue his faith and observe the Torah. He who can not leave the country either because of the danger of sea travel or for some other good reason, ought at least not profane the name of God. He ought to continue to observe the

Jewish law secretly. God will double his reward because he exposed himself to danger.

This remarkable letter was written by Maimonides when he was not yet thirty years of age.[10] It shows that Maimonides felt not only the anguish of the entire Jewish community because of the attack of some fanatics, but voiced also the suffering of his own family.

Thus he encouraged the Jews of Morocco to continue their Judaism secretly and thereby saved the entire community. Incidentally he set forth a new philosophy of Judaism applicable in times of forced apostasy: Jews may utter a formula of acceptance of another religion for the sake of saving their lives, provided they are not compelled to transgress the Jewish law. A Jew who accepts another religion by *force majeure*, is to be considered, according to the law, a religious Jew.

Maimun's family lived in Fez in this strained atmosphere. Moses ben Maimun continued his work on the Mishna, with the encouragement of the Rabbi of Fez, Judah ibn Shoshan, and also pursued his study of medicine under the guidance of Arabic physicians. Although he observed Jewish law in its entirety, he disguised himself as a native. It is probable that during the month of Ramadan (ninth month of the Mohammedan year) he even joined in the Tarawith prayers. Since he did not consider the Moslems as idolatrous, nor the Mosque a house of idolatry, he could enter a Mosque even during Ramadan, without violating his conscience as a loyal Jew. In one of his responsa, in fact, he clearly expressed the view that the Moslems were not to be considered idolatrous, for they believed in the Unity of God and their conception of His Unity was without any flaw.[11]

About the year 1165, Rabbi Judah ibn Shoshan, the most eminent Rabbi of Fez, was seized by the Moslems and executed. Maimonides was now fearful that he would share the same fate as his friend and teacher. Very likely he had been already caught in the net of Almohades, but had been saved from death only by the intervention of his Moslem friend, the poet and theologian, Abul Arab ibn Moisha.

Deciding to flee from the country, he embarked on a Saturday night on the fourth of the month of Iyar, in the year 1165, for Palestine, which was then a Christian country called the Kingdom of Jerusalem. Maimonides' own account of his stormy voyage to the Holy Land is revelatory of his religious instincts. "On the evening of the first day of the week, the fourth of the month Iyar, I went to sea, and on Sabbath the tenth of Iyar, of the year 25, we had a dreadful storm; the sea was in a fury and we were in danger of perishing. Then I vowed to keep these two days as complete fast days for myself and my household, and all those connected with me, and to command my children to do the same throughout all their generations; they should also give charity according to their ability. For myself I further vowed to remain apart from human intercourse on every 10th of Iyar, to speak to nobody and only to pray and to study, as on that day I saw no one on the sea except the Holy One, praised be His name, so will I see no one and stay with no one on that day in the years to come. On the evening of the first day of the week, the 3rd of Sivan, I landed safely and came to Acco, and by arriving in the land of Israel, I escaped persecution. This day I vowed to keep as a day of rejoicing, festivity, and distribution of charity, for myself and my house throughout all generations."[12]

While he was in Palestine, he continued his work, the commentary on the Mishna. He associated himself with the rabbis of the country, particularly with Rabbi Japhet of Acco, with whom he became very friendly.

For the first time, he lived in a country under Christian domination. His contact with the Christians evidently did not impress him very much. One can readily understand the reason, for the hands of the Crusaders who killed many Jews during the year 1147, were still reeking with the blood of their victims. He regarded the images of Jesus and Mary, and the statues of the different Saints, before whom the Christians kneeled and prayed, as idols. He, therefore, considered the Christians to be different from the Moslems and put them in the category of idol worshippers who did not believe in the Unity of God.[13] In the short time that he was in Acco, he apparently did not associate with the Knights and the Ministers of the church to learn more about Christianity. Upon leaving the country, there remained with him the impression that they were heathens. Even though the Christians believed in the Bible and accepted the five books of Moses as well as the prophets as Holy, inspired by the Divine Spirit, he considered them idolatrous, classifying them in his Halakic work among idol worshippers.

He finally decided to leave for Egypt; he did not think Palestine was the proper place for him to reside. At that time there were very few Jews in Palestine, for after the first Crusade most of them were either killed or compelled to flee from the country. The few that remained were impoverished and deficient in culture. He could not find the requisite stimulus for work among Jews or Christians in Palestine.

Before leaving for Egypt he undertook a trip on the fourth day of Marheshvan in the year 4926 (the autumn of 1165) to Jerusalem. He tells us that this journey was fraught with great danger. This was undoubtedly true for Amalric I was then the King of Jerusalem and tolerated no Jews in his domain. Maimonides gives a fairly detailed account of his pilgrimages to Jerusalem. He says: "I entered the great and the Holy place and prayed there on the 6th of the same month. On the first day of the following week, being the 9th, I left Jerusalem and went to Hebron, in order to kiss the graves of the patriarchs in the cave. On that day, I stood in the cave and prayed: Thanks be to the Father of all for everything! The two days, the 6th and 9th of Marheshvan, I designated by a vow as festivals devoted to solemn prayer and festivity. May God give me strength and assist me to fulfill my vows; and may I and all Israel soon be permitted to see the land in its glory, even as I prayed there in its state of desolation! Amen."[14]

It is very singular that Maimonides does not mention

his father at all in the account of his journey from Morocco to Egypt. He writes as if he himself were the head of the family. Is there a likelihood that Maimun, the father of Moses, remained in Palestine or even Morocco?

Maimonides, we may safely surmise, went back from Hebron to Acco and sailed from there to Egypt. It would be too dangerous a trip for him to take the road from Hebron to Egypt through the desert, as the presence of many crusaders made it almost impossible for a Jew to travel. We may assume, therefore, that he sailed from Acco to Alexandria, Egypt, sometime toward the end of the year 1165 or at the beginning of the year 1166. At that time the Kingdom of Jerusalem was negotiating with the Egyptians, and the fleet of the Kingdom of Jerusalem was anchored at the port of Alexandria against the invasion of Nureddin, the Sultan of Syria.[15]

just as the Karaites did with respect to the Bible and oral traditions.

When Maimonides arrived in Alexandria, either in 1165 or 1166, the Jewish community was in a chaotic state. The Nagid Samuel had died in the year 1159.[3] Not long before his death, he had been denounced as a traitor to the Caliph by a fellow-Jew, Yahya-Zuta, who had aspired to the office of Nagid. Zuta had succeeded in removing Samuel from office for sixty-six days. It is very likely that Samuel had been arrested and put in jail in chains (Zuta later had even succeeded to the office of Nagid). But, shortly before his death, Samuel had been reinstated. After his death, no successor had been appointed.[4]

When Maimonides arrived in Egypt, he did not look for a rabbinical position, since he greatly disapproved of scholars who lived by their scholarship and made their learning a source of income. He believed that a scholar should live like the ordinary man by the toil of his hands. He felt that the public would never respect a scholar or his scholarship, if he derived his livelihood from his learning. He saw no objection, however, to a learned man investing his money with a partner and sharing the profits.[5] Scholarship, however, must never be made a business. Furthermore, being independent by nature, he would not accept a position which would make him a possible pliant tool in the hands of leaders.

The Jewish community of Alexandria and all the Jews of Egypt during that period, were not highly cultivated; even the rabbis left no mark of scholarship among the Jews of the world. They were far inferior to the Jews of Spain. There were no rabbis of such eminence as ibn Migas, or poets such as Judah Halevi, ibn Gabirol or ibn Ezra. Maimonides would never accept a position in such a community. He knew quite well that if he wanted to have any influence over the masses, he must not be subservient to them. It seems that Maimonides never considered Egypt as his adopted country. Even at the height of his glory in Egypt, he never signed his name Moses of Egypt but always Moses the Spaniard. In Alexandria, he continued his scholarly research, while his brother David who was engaged in the jewelry trade was the support of the family.[6]

IV

THE COMMENTARY ON THE MISHNA

AT THE age of thirty-three, in the year 1168, Maimonides brought to completion his commentary on the Mishna, *Saraj* (the Luminary), which he had begun in 1158 while he lived in Cordova. He had to labor at this commentary under great hardships during his exile and while travelling in different countries and crossing the sea. He, therefore, begged his readers for leniency in case they found any errors.[1]

The purpose of the commentary, as he himself said, was to interpret the word as well as the text of the Mishna, because to understand this code one must know the entire Talmud by heart—a task which is practically impossible, particularly when a Halacha is interpreted in different places in the Talmud. He, therefore, found it necessary to interpret the Mishna according to the Talmud. He made an effort also to give the decision of the Law. He next presented an introduction to the student who wanted to study the Talmud. Finally, he gave to the reader who was familiar with the Talmud, a ready guide and a digest of it.

In this commentary on the Mishna, he presented the Halacha in such a manner as to make it easy for a student to understand the difficult passages in the Talmud. He wrote introductions to every section of the Mishna, particularly to the last, the sixth, "*Tohorot,*" in which he described the different laws of purity and impurity, usually considered the most complicated laws in the Talmud. It has been said that if the Rambam had left us only this introduction, his name would remain one of the greatest in Jewish history.[2]

In the introduction to the first section, he outlined the history of Jewish tradition. He divided all Jewish laws into five divisions:

The first contains the interpretation of the laws that were handed down by Moses, and are implied in the Bible, or may be deduced by logical argument. Concerning the validity of these laws no controversies can arise.

The second division includes the laws which are designated as the laws of Moses from Mount Sinai.

In the third group are the laws which have been deduced by legal argument on which controversies have arisen. Such laws have always been decided according to the opinion of the majority.

The fourth division contains the laws which the prophets and the sages instituted to make a fence around the Torah. These are the different decrees which are recorded in the Talmud.

In the fifth group are the laws which have become such by agreement of the rabbis. These are called *Takkana* and *Minhag.*

In this introduction also appears a catalogue and genealogy of all the scholars from the early period of the Talmud, from Simon the Just up to Rabbi Judah, the compiler of the Mishna.

Maimonides, in his commentary on the Mishna gave not only the decision of the Halacha as interpreted in the Talmud, but also found occasion for expounding his philosophy of Judaism. In the tractate, *Sanhedrin,* in the commentary on the tenth chapter where the Mishna reads, "All Israelites have a share in the *Olam Haba*" (the future world), he ventured a solution to the questions, "What is Life to Come?" and "Who is an Israelite?"

He said that many Jews had a wrong conception of the "Life to Come." He instanced those who believed that Paradise—*Gan-Eden*—was a place where the rivers were running with wine and where people ate and drank, free from toil and where they had beautiful homes. These credulous people also believed that Gehenna, "Hell," was a place where the bodies of wicked men would be burned and tortured. They tried to find support for their belief in the Scriptures. Another group held that the reward of the righteous would be life in the Messianic age when they would be like angels, gigantic in their stature and immortal, and when they would be provided with garments ready to be worn and food already prepared to be eaten. This group also held that the wicked would not be permitted to witness this Messianic age. The third group had a different conception of reward. They believed that the righteous would be resurrected after death, to live again with their families and dear ones, eating and drinking with them, and that they would never die a second time. This group like the others also tried to base its belief upon the sayings of the sages and the Scriptures. The fourth group held that the reward derived from following the divine Law would be happiness and pleasure in this world resulting from the possession of wealth, children, good health and security. They also believed that the Jews would have their own Kingdom and would rule over all those responsible for their sufferings, but that the Jews who did not observe the Precepts would suffer here on this earth. The fifth group was a very large one who entertained the combined notions of the other four groups. They maintained that the world to come meant the time when Messiah would appear, when the dead would be resurrected, and, assembled in the garden of Eden, would eat and drink, and enjoy health for eternity.

Maimonides saw that none of these groups had a proper conception of "Olam Haba." These people were interested in knowing in what clothing the dead would arise, whether in the beautiful embroidered shrouds in which they were buried or in some simple garments. These people showed great eagerness to know whether upon the arrival of the Messiah, there would be rich and poor, strong and weak. And they asked other questions like these.

Maimonides classified these people into three categories. The first, which composed the great majority

to be ideal, but they had to be resorted to since the child could not fully comprehend the significance of his studies. Similar inducements had to be offered to the average man who did not fully understand the importance of observing the Precepts. Since his philosophy of life was to do nothing, unless he derives benefit or escapes a loss by his act, he must be promised some reward. One cannot tell an average man to practice the Precepts for their own sake. He would be bewildered and not understand. Only a man like Abraham did things without thought of reward. The rabbis, therefore, were justified in saying to the masses that they would be rewarded if they observed the Precepts and that they would be punished if they did not. Thus they encourage the masses to observe the Jewish law. The people however, who observed the Laws suffered no loss because they were induced to observe the Precepts, and they might in the end, serve God, without any selfish motives.

Maimonides then presented his own conception of *Olam Haba. Olam Haba,* he said, was not a place where people ate and drank or enjoyed any other earthly pleasures, but a place where the righteous sat with the crowns on their heads and enjoyed the divine glory, their souls thus had full comprehension of the truth of the Creator, just like the Angels who enjoy intense happiness in what they understand of His existence. The goal was to reach the highest society, a goal to which no pleasure could be compared and to which no reward could be likened. The punishment of the wicked consisted in the destruction of their souls; they would never reach the place where the righteous sat and enjoyed the divine glory. Moreover, the prophets themselves stated that *Olam Haba* could not be comprehended with the bodily senses. The rabbis, likewise, said that all the prophets prophesied the Messianic Age, but *Olam Haba* nobody ever apprehended but God, Himself.[4]

Maimonides did not deny the possibility of Paradise being a most wonderful place where there were many rivers and beautiful trees bearing all kinds of fruits or the possibility of such a place being accessible to people for their enjoyment. Who knows but there might be many species of new plants there of which we had never known. Probably Gehenna was a place where the wicked were tortured, but the Talmud does not specify the nature of their punishment.[5] Some people believe that the sun will come out so strong that its rays will burn the wicked.

Maimonides then took up the question of Resurrection. Resurrection was one of the principles of the Torah. The righteous only and not the wicked were resurrected. One thing was clear; man after death had to return to the form in which he was composed. He, however, did not as yet fully expound his views on *Olam Haba*, and Resurrection. He did not specify definitely whether there was a bodily Resurrection.

He entered upon a complete exposition of his theories on the subject of the Messianic Age. It meant for Maimonides, the time when the Jews would return to Palestine and have their own Kingdom. The King Messiah would be a greater king than Solomon but no appreciable difference in the nature of this world would occur. There would be no Utopia. Then, as now, rich and poor, strong and weak, would continue to exist side by side but people would find it easier than in our day to wrest a livelihood from the soil for it would be fertile and fruitful. The Messiah would be mortal like ordinary man, and his son would rule after him, and so on, his descendants ruling. His Kingdom would last long in his own lifetime, for the span of life would lengthen because people, without having to worry or to suffer, would live to a greater age. Jews do not look forward to the Messianic Age because they will have better dwellings, or because they will ride on wonderful horses and drink good wine, as many people believe. The Messianic Age will differ from the present time only in that the Jews will be in possession of their own country, where they will be able to study and observe the Torah.

After he expounded his philosophy on *Olam Haba* (The World to Come) and presented his views as to the Messiah and the Messianic Age, he gave his definition of the Israelite who would have a share in the Olam Haba and of the heretic who would not have a share in the "World to Come." He formulated thirteen articles of faith which every Jew had to accept. These were:

1. Belief in the existence of a Creator who is the cause of all creations.
2. Belief in the Unity of God.
3. Belief in His incorporeality, for of God no substance could be predicated.

4. Belief that He has no beginning and that He is eternal.
5. Belief that He is our Master and that we must worship Him alone.
6. Belief in prophecy.
7. Belief that there was no Prophet like Moses and that there never would be another like him.
8. Belief that the Law which was given to Moses on Mount Sinai came in its entirety from God.
9. Belief in the eternity and immutability of the Law.
10. Belief that God knows the acts and ways of man.
11. Belief that God would reward the righteous and punish the wicked.
12. Belief in the coming of Messiah.
13. Belief in the resurrection of the dead.

Maimonides was the first to formulate thirteen principles of Judaism. In his time, when the Jews lived all over the known globe of that day, and no central authority existed, it was almost presumptuous for a young man to declare that a Jew who does not believe in one of these thirteen principles would not share in the World to Come. Especially bold was his assertion that a Jew who believes that God is corporeal is to be considered a heretic. It is well known that in his day many rabbis of great learning held the opinion that God could be conceived as corporeal. His theory which he later incorporated in his Mishne Torah, aroused the ire of many of the great rabbis. His thirteen principles of Judaism were generally accepted but not without opposition,[6] and later they were included in the synagogue ritual. The well known hymn, "Yigdal", which is chanted in many synagogues, is a metrical reading of his thirteen principles.

In his introduction to the tractate *Abot* which deals with the ethics of the sages, he found occasion to set forth a special treatise on psychology and ethics, known as the *Eight Chapters.*[7] In these *Eight Chapters*, he introduced Hellenistic ideas into Judaism. He based his ethics on the sayings of the sages and on the Aristotelian principles in the *Nicomachean Ethics*. He introduced his thesis in the first two chapters where he dealt with physiological conceptions. He compared the ethical teacher to the physician. Just as a physician must know the body and its anatomy to be able to cure a person and administer proper remedies, so must the moralist have a proper knowledge of the soul in its entirety and in its parts, to heal it and to perfect one's moral qualities. He must know how to prevent the soul from becoming diseased and how to maintain its health.[8]

In chapters three and four, he dealt with the diseases of the soul and their cures. He followed the theories of the philosophers who held that the soul, like the body, was capable of enjoying health and suffering illness. As a person who is physically ill finds that sweet tastes bitter and bitter tastes sweet, so the person whose soul is ill, that is, he who is wicked and morally perverted, mistakenly regards bad as good and good as bad. Maimonides went on to say, that just as a man who is sick bodily and unfamiliar with the science of medicine consults a physician and learns often that he must avoid things he himself considered beneficial in order to be cured, so a person whose soul is sick should consult the sage, the moral physician, who will advise for him a cure against indulging in those evils which he (whose soul is ill) thinks are good. However, the person who is morally out of joint but not aware of the fact, thinking he is morally sound, or who realizes that he needs spiritual aid, but does not seek it, is in the same position as one who is ill in body, and, neglecting to consult a physician for a cure, runs the risk of the consequences of continued indulgence of himself. Such a course must surely result in an untimely death.[9]

In chapter four, Maimonides, taking Aristotle for his guide, maintained that the acts of man should always be evenly balanced. He should not go to one extreme or another but adjust his deeds to the proper mean.[10]

In chapter five, he laid down the principle based on the dictum of the sages, "let all your actions be for the sake of God,"[11] that the aim of man in life was to understand God.

In chapter six, he reconciled the views of the Greek philosophers and those of the Jewish sages on the question as to which was the superior, the saintly man who had no desires or inclinations to do evil, or the man who had to subdue his evil inclinations in order to lead an upright life. The philosophers maintained that the natural saint was superior to and more perfect than he who had to struggle for rectitude,[12] while the sages maintained the reverse.[13] To bridge a gap between these two points of view, Maimonides asserted that the philosophers had given a prior position to the saint because he never experienced a tendency to commit such crimes as murder, stealing, etc., for a person who has the desire to commit such crimes is certainly imperfect.

The sages agreed with the philosophers that any man who desired to murder but refrained from doing so was inferior to one who had not the desire to commit such a crime. When the sages put on a higher plane those who overcame their inclinations, they meant those who overcame their desire to transgress ceremonial laws such as the partaking of milk and meat together. People who curbed such temptations were superior to those who never had any thought of violating the ceremonial laws.

In chapter seven, he dealt with the subject of prophets.

In chapter eight, he concerned himself chiefly with the problem of providence and he subjected the pseudoscience of astrology to severe criticism. He dealt with all these problems at length in his later works, both in *Sefer-Ha-Mada* the first book of his Mishne Torah, and in his *Moreh Nebuchim* (The Guide for the Perplexed).

The Eight Chapters which were written like the rest of the commentary on the Mishna in Arabic were translated into Hebrew by Samuel ibn Tibbon, possibly in the year 1202, in the lifetime of Maimonides.[14]

Maimonides, in his commentary on the Mishna, availed himself of every occasion to advance his own views. He condemned many different customs and habits in vogue at that time among the Jews. In his commentary on *Sotah* he bitterly denounced the people who used to inscribe the name of God in amulets. In his commentary on *Bekhoroth* he laid down his conviction that no scholar should make his scholarship a source of income but should engage in useful work or commerce. He stressed his belief that the scholars were the chosen of mankind and insisted that they should be entitled to special privileges such as exemption from taxation on their land. He likewise opposed the custom of the Jews in giving priority in the call to the Torah to a priest who was an *Am Ha-Arez*, over one of non-priestly stock who was a scholar.

In many cases, Maimonides even contested the decisions of the Gaonim. He was indeed independent and courageous when he said, "Such was the opinion of the Gaonim but they did not fully comprehend these principles" or when he said, "So the Gaonim have decided but I am of a different opinion."[15]

Since this commentary was written not for the scholar but primarily for the layman and for rabbis who did not possess great scholarship on complicated Talmudic subjects, he called the attention of the reader to the summing up by admonishing him, and saying, "Remember this principle and do not compel me to repeat it." Or he told him to keep in mind the topic under discussion and endeavor to understand the interpretation he gave of important principles, particularly when many of the Gaonim did not fully grasp the subject.[16]

We can determine from internal evidence when and where some of his commentaries were written. Since he

V

AFFAIRS IN EGYPT

WHILE Maimonides was busy writing his commentary and at the same time was engaged in the study of medicine, Egypt underwent a revolution. On the fourth day of August, 1167, a treaty had been signed between Amalrick, the King of Jerusalem and Shirkuh, the Vizier of Nureddin, the Sultan of Damascus, in which they agreed not to molest Egypt.[1] The King of Jerusalem entered upon the treaty for the purpose of obtaining a free hand to prepare for an attack on Damascus. His counsellors advised him to conquer Egypt first. In the beginning he sought to disregard their counsel since an attack upon Egypt exposed him to an assault from Nureddin. He maintained that an attack upon Egypt would throw Shawar, the Vizier, into the arms of Nureddin. His objections were in vain, and he made the first attack upon Egypt in the year 1168, on the third of November. Bilbeys was captured and a wholesale massacre was carried out in which neither age nor sex was spared.[2] This barbarous act at once made the Egyptians conclude that their safety lay only in allying themselves with Nureddin. Shawar, the Vizier, sent an embassy to Damascus to implore Nureddin's aid. In the meantime, to delay the attack against Egypt, he gave orders to set the entire city of Fostat on fire so that it should not afford shelter to the army of the King of Jerusalem. It will be recalled that in 1812 Kutusov, Commander-in-Chief of the Russian army, followed a similar plan in connection with Moscow where he had to retreat before the invasion of Bonaparte and thus saved Russia.

In response to Shawar's appeal, Nureddin came to aid the Egyptians, sending an army under the leadership of the Vizier, Shirkuh, and his nephew Saladin. Saladin was not very anxious to march again into Egypt to defend her from the invaders. However, under the pressure of his uncle Shirkuh, he followed him to Egypt. On January 8, 1169, Shirkuh and Shawar combined their forces against the army of Amalric, the King of Jerusalem. Amalrick regarded it a more prudent policy to retreat to Palestine without giving battle to the allies.

Shirkuh triumphantly entered Cairo and was received by the inhabitants with great jubilation. Shawar, who had asked the Sultan of Damascus to send an army to help him against the Crusaders, now became envious of Shirkuh and schemed to get rid of him. His plan became known to the Syrians and reached the ears of Saladin who determined to frustrate it and dispose of Shawar. So when Shawar one day entered the camp of the Syrians, Saladin arrested him. When the news of his arrest reached the Caliph el Adid, instead of demanding the release of his Vizier he asked that the head of Shawar be sent to him. He was happy that the Syrians delivered him from a Vizier who had dominated him.

point of death. A few days after this revolution, he died, and Saladin now became the Viceroy of Egypt.[5]

This revolution in the year 1171 induced Maimonides to leave Alexandria for Fostat where he was to remain the rest of his life. There were several reasons for his migration to Fostat. After finishing his commentary on the Mishna, he had intensively studied medicine and other sciences. Fostat was a more suitable place for him since Saladin established schools there for higher learning.

His migration may also be explained by economic reasons. The family of Maimonides found it hazardous to conduct their jewelry business with Moslem countries that could be reached only by the Mediterranean Sea. This sea was no longer safe for Egyptian vessels since the combined fleet of the King of Jerusalem and of his allies could always harass them, particularly since the fleet was besieging Damietta a short distance from Alexandria. Cairo, situated on the Nile and not far from the Red Sea, was more advantageous for the business interests of Maimonides' family. It is also likely that Cairo, being the Capital, the place where the women of the Caliph's harem resided, offered a better market for jewelry than Alexandria. Fostat had also been rebuilt since Saladin became Vizier and its former inhabitants had returned there.

When Maimonides arrived in Fostat, Zuta was the Nagid. Having obtained his position from Saladin by bribery, and being responsible for the downfall of the

Nagid Samuel, he was hated and opposed by many Jews. Zuta called himself Sar-Shalom. The Jews, however, named him Shor-Shalom (a complete ox).[6] Maimonides shared their animosity and joined them in their opposition to Zuta.

by creating a new religion similar to the Jewish religion.

Their efforts to do this would not succeed. One of these new religions had now only gentiles as adherents and it did not cause any harm to Judaism itself; yet the originator of this religion, Jesus, had no intention of spreading his religion among the gentiles.[1a] Another man (Mohammed) arose who also like Jesus sought to destroy the Jewish religion by creating a new religion similar to it. The difference between this new leader and his predecessor was that he tried to obtain political power and rule over the nations of the world. Maimonides said that anyone could understand the truth of the Jewish religion and detect the falsity of the other two religions.

He advised his fellow Jews of Yemen not to become discouraged by persecution which could not last forever. God had already promised Jacob that his children, the Jews, would remain while the nations who persecuted them would disappear. Maimonides appealed to the Jews of Yemen as follows: "Strengthen yourselves and let not the persecution frighten you because that is only a test from God to see how strong your faith in Him is." He gave the same advice to them that he gave to the Jews of Fez, to leave the country when one could afford to do so. He thus argued with them: If a man cannot make a living in one place, he tries to go elsewhere where he can find better opportunities. Certainly, if a person cannot observe the Torah in one locality, he should go to another where he will be able to observe it.

Maimonides then confuted the arguments of the renegade who maintained that the Bible had referred to Mohammed in the passage where it is written, "The Lord thy God will raise up unto thee a prophet from the midst of thee, of thy brethren, like unto me." Maimonides interpreted the words to mean that the prophet who would rise in Israel would be one of their own brethren, and not an outsider. As to the verse, "I will multiply him exceedingly" which the renegade said referred to Mohammed because the numerical value of the letters of the Hebrew word for "exceedingly" was ninety-two and the numerical value of the Hebrew letters for Mohammed was also ninety-two, Maimonides maintained that the word for "exceedingly" could not refer to Mohammed for since it was accompanied by the word "multiply," the latter word implied quantity and did not designate quality.

As to the time when the Messiah would appear, Maimonides said that, though Saadia Gaon had ventured to set a date, one could not know this with certainty for the time was not revealed to any person. Many sages were opposed to calculating the date of the Messiah. One had to exonerate Saadia for his calculations, although he knew it was not permitted, on the ground that his generation was of low intellectual standing when the Torah was almost forgotten. Saadia saw fit to encourage the Jews in this way by fixing the date of the arrival of the Messiah; he certainly meant well.

Maimonides mentioned another man in Spain who not many years before wrote a book in which he foretold

inflict severe punishment upon him. He realized the dangers of writing such a letter but when so important a request was made of him, he set at naught his personal safety.

Thus, in this letter he tried to persuade the Yemenite Jews to remain faithful to Judaism since persecutions would never destroy the Jews; and he showed them that, on the contrary the oppressors are destroyed, and cited illustrations from history.

The Jews of Yemen followed the advice of Maimonides, uncomplainingly bore their suffering and remained loyal to the Jewish religion. The persecutions did not last long, for in the year 1174, Turan Shah, the brother of Saladin, conquered Yemen[4] and delivered the Jews from the fanatics. They now enjoyed such religious freedom as did the Jews in Egypt. Economic, as well as spiritual conditions, changed for the better. Maimonides was now idolized in Yemen; he became the most popular person there. In the daily sanctification prayers (Kaddish) a special prayer was inserted for the welfare of Moses ben Maimun.[5] We may assume that this epistle also gave him great prestige in Egypt, the country of his adoption.

The epistle to Yemen presented Maimonides' views on the most important principles of Judaism. He believed that the age when the Jews were suffering so painfully throughout the world, in Europe from the Crusaders, in Andalusia from the Almohades, in Morocco and now in Yemen, was the time of the "Agony of Messiah." He furthermore believed that the conquest of the world by the Cross and the Crescent, heralded the period of the Messianic Age. One sees from this letter, also, that Maimonides believed that before the advent of the Messiah, a prophet would arise in Palestine who would be primarily a scholar. Maimonides objected very strongly to the scholars who insisted in giving the date of the appearance of the Messiah. Yet, he himself committed the same act when he said that a prophet would arise in the year four thousand nine hundred and seventy-six of the creation. A number of biographers of Maimonides, however, believe that a passage so inconsistent with his views is spurious.[6] Others maintain that the Jews were so insistent on knowing the exact date of the coming of the Messiah that even Maimonides succumbed to the universal demand and followed the general practice of giving the Messianic date.[7]

Neither of these theories is correct, there is no contradiction in the letter. He condemned others for giving the date of the arrival of the Messiah and he did not do so himself. What he did do was to give the year when prophecy would reveal itself in Israel. Although he believed that his age was the period of agony through which the Jews had to go before the coming of the Messiah, he was careful not to give the date of that future event. But he did the next best thing, for believing the new revelation of prophecy would precede the coming of the Messiah, he fixed the time of the prophetic revelation. We must bear in mind that he believed the prophet would be a scholar and that the Messiah would not be a

VII

ESTABLISHMENT OF THE EXILARCHATE IN EGYPT

MAIMONIDES, in the course of his letter to Rabbi Japhet of Acco, had complained that informers were trying to destroy him. Most likely he referred to the Nagid Zuta against whom he had joined the opposition. Maimonides feared that Zuta would inform the government that he lived in Morocco disguised as a Moslem. Such information, of course, would endanger his life. Maimonides had cause for his anxiety since Zuta had previously been instrumental in having the Nagid Samuel imprisoned by reporting him to the authorities.

In the mid seventies of the twelfth century, the opposition against the Nagid Zuta succeeded in removing him from his position. The Nagiduth, the office of Nagid, was temporarily abolished in Egypt. The victory which the opposition won over the Nagid was not due to their own strength but rather to the political circumstances then existing in Egypt.

Although Saladin became the Viceroy of Egypt after the death of the Caliph el Adid, he was still a subordinate of Nureddin, the Sultan of Damascus. Saladin, who had planned to make himself independent of Damascus, had reason to fear that Nureddin would not allow him to establish himself permanently in Egypt. Anticipating an attack from Nureddin, he sought to conquer Yemen, Mecca and other places so that he should be able to retreat to some distant haven of safety in case of invasion. Nureddin would, undoubtedly, grasp the first opportunity to seize Egypt and become ruler of a powerful domain extending from the North to the South, and thus be in a position to encircle the Franks in Palestine and put an end to the Kingdom of Jerusalem.

However, Nureddin died in May, 1174,[1] before he had the opportunity of making an attack upon Saladin. His son, Salih Ismail, who was still a child, eleven years old, now came to the throne. But as a matter of fact there was no real leader in Syria to succeed him. Many of the subordinate states declared their independence of Damascus. Disunion and anarchy prevailed. The governor of Mosul, who was the young king Salih's cousin, annexed Edessa and other states of Syria. The Emir of Aleppo kidnapped the child King from Damascus to his realm. The Franks now had the opportunity of realizing the dream of Amalrick to capture Damascus, annex it to the Kingdom of Jerusalem, and then conquer Egypt. But Amalrick also died at the time of Nureddin's death and likewise left a son thirteen years of age, a leper. Baldwin, one of the military leaders of the Kingdom of Jerusalem, who recently had been freed by Nureddin from captivity, became the Regent of the boy King. Thus, the Kingdom of Jerusalem like Damascus was also ruled by a child King.

Photo by Emanuel Hoschander

PAGE FROM MAIMONIDES' MISHNE TORAH, BOOK II, COLOGNE 1295

VIII

MISHNE TORAH—THE JEWISH CONSTITUTION

In 1180, Maimonides completed his *Magnum Opus*, the *Mishne Torah* (The Second Torah) or as it is known *Yad Ha-Hasakah* (Strong Hand). Written in Mishnaic Hebrew, it comprised all the Biblical laws and other laws and customs in existence up to his own time. This work divided into fourteen books, was completed after ten years of enormous labor. Each book dealt with several topics of Jewish law.

The first book "*Sefer Ha-Mada*" (The Book of Knowledge) deals with the principles of Judaism. Since the knowledge of the Law is indispensable for a study of the Jewish religion, he included the laws of the study of the Torah.

The second book "*Sefer Ahabah*" (The Book of Love) enumerates all the laws connected with the Precepts which it is incumbent upon a Jew to observe such as those relating to prayers, reading of the *Shema* and the laws of Phylacteries. The laws of Circumcision are also herein included.

The third book, "*Zemanim*" (Seasons) treats of the Precepts like the laws of Sabbath and the Festivals which must be observed at a definite time.

Having set out in detail the Precepts which a man must regularly observe, he sets forth also the laws for the observance of which there is usually only a single occasion in a lifetime. These include the laws of Marriage which he presents in the next book, the fourth, "*Nashim*" (Women). Here he also deals with Divorce and Levirate Marriage.

He follows with Book Five, in which he demonstrates the laws of Prohibited Marriages and also lays down the laws connected with Forbidden Foods. This book is called "*Kedushah*" (Sanctification).

Following the order in the Mishna, he takes up in the sixth book, "*Haflaah*" (Separation) the laws of Vows, of Oaths, and the Nazarite.

After detailing the laws relating to the person, he sets forth the laws relating to agriculture, and those connected with the Sabbatical year and the different Tithes given to the priests and Levites serving in the Temple. This book is called "*Zeraim*" (Seeds).

In the following book, the eighth, "*Abodah*" (Worship) he sets forth the laws relating to the Temple, the divine services and the communal sacrifices.

Logically connected with the laws of sacrifices are those dealing with individual sacrifices. He therefore treats of these in the next book, the ninth, which he calls "*Korbanot*" (Sacrifices).

Since he gave all the laws connected with Sanctity, he set forth in the tenth book, which is called "*Tohorah*" (Purification), those relating to purity and impurity.

After having given the laws between man and God,

he gives in the following book, the eleventh, called "*Nezikin*" (Damages) the laws between man and man, such as those relating to Theft, Robbery, various damages, Injuries and Homicide.

He continues writing on the laws between man and man in the twelfth book, "*Kinyan*" (Possession) where he states the laws of Sale, Possession, Partnership and Agency. He also included the laws of Slavery in this book since slaves were considered real property.

The thirteenth book, "*Mishpatim*" (Judgements) treats of the laws connected with the claims of litigants which may arise after Sale and Possession. In the same book he includes the different laws of Credit.

Finally, in the fourteenth book, he gives the laws connected with Testimony, with Judges, the procedure of the court and the sentence the judges should pronounce. In the same book he includes the laws relating to disobedience by members of the court and rebellion against Judaism which are generally punishable by death. Hence, he gives the laws of Mourning in this book. He then takes up the principles of government and gives the laws relating to the King and the State as well as regulations concerning war. He concludes with the laws in reference to the return of the Jews to Palestine under the King Messiah. This last book, he names "*Shoftim*" (Judges).

In a short introduction, Maimonides stated that all the commandments as well as their interpretations were given to Moses on Mount Sinai. The Torah was the written law while *Mitzvah* was the interpretation and was called the Oral Law. Then he related the history of the tradition and listed all the sages from Moses to Rabbi Judah, the Nasi, the compiler of the Mishna,[1] mentioning by name the more important ones from Rabbi Judah, the Nasi, up to Rav Ashi, the compiler of the Gemara. He enumerated forty generations, from Moses to Rav Ashi.

The Babylonian Gemara was compiled one hundred years after the compilation of the Palestinian Gemara. The two Gemaras contain the interpretation of the Mishnayot, and all the laws which were enacted in the different academies from the days of Rabbi Judah to the time of their compilation. Then came the Gaonim who wrote treatises in explanation of each Gemara. Some of them interpreted individual laws while others interpreted chapters, sections or tractates. Some Gaonim wrote independent treatises on the Law.

"In our days," said Maimonides, "when scholars are few and scholarship rare, I, Moses, the son of Maimon the Spaniard, am compiling a book on the entire Jewish Law without discussions or debates, wherein all the laws are clearly explained." He claimed in short that his book included all the laws from the Bible down to the compilation of the Gemaras as they were interpreted by the Gaonim. He even contended that it was not necessary to consult any other work except his for a knowledge of the Jewish Law. "Therefore," he said, "I call this book Mishne Torah (The Second Torah)." He indited this introduction in the year 4937 A.M.,

1177 C.E., after he had completed a great part of his work and seven years after he had begun it.

In the first book, *Sefer ha-Mada,* he codified the laws relating to the thirteen principles of Judaism, which he had already formulated in his commentary on the Mishna. He considered any Jew who did not believe in any of the thirteen principles a heretic. He named five different categories of men whom he called *minim* (heretics). First, there were those who maintained there was no God, second, those who did not believe in the unity of God, third, those who maintained that God was corporeal, fourth, those who said that God did not create the world *ex nihilo,* and fifth, those who worshipped stars and planets. Since he placed among the heretics those who believed that the Creator was corporeal, he aroused the ire of great rabbis of that period as was alluded to in a previous chapter. The conception that God was corporeal was very popular among the Jews for many centuries. Maimonides thus excluded a great percentage of the Jewish people and also many prominent rabbis from the *Olam Haba* (The World to Come). Rabbi Abraham ben David of Posquieres, in his *Hassagot* (Criticism) on the Mishne Torah, very vigorously objected to Maimonides' doctrine and expressed himself thus: "Greater and better people than he believe in this idea."[2]

Maimonides also named three categories of Jews whom he called *Apicursim,* Epicureans. First, those who maintained that there was no prophecy, second, those who denied the prophecy of Moses, and third, those who believed that God did not know the acts of man. This list of those who would not share in the *Olam Haba* was not exclusive.

He dealt at length with the problems of Free-will and Providence. He regarded intellect as the most perfect possession of man by which he could avoid committing evil acts and indulging in wicked thoughts. He enumerated all the laws relating to idolatry in which he included astrology. He gave the laws connected with the study of the Torah and those relative to scholars and scholarship. He also set forth the laws connected with the writing of a Sefer Torah (Holy Scroll).

He gave the order of the daily prayers, and those of the Sabbath and different Holidays, at the end of the second book. It is worthy of note that he did not include the prayer of *Kol Nidre* in the liturgy of the Day of Atonement.

In the remaining books, he set forth the rest of the laws. He divided them in two definite classes, the laws in the Bible and the laws which were handed down by *Soferim* (Scribes). He regarded as Biblical not only the laws which are numerated in the Torah but those derived from them by the *Soferim* by analogy. He also considered as Biblical all the laws which the rabbis had by tradition assigned to Moses and he called them *Mfi-H'Shmuah.* He regarded all the laws which were introduced by the sages through *Midoth,* i.e. logical arguments, as rabbinical and not Biblical.

We may illustrate Maimonides' view as to what is Biblical and what is rabbinical by a few illustrations.

According to the Mishna, a woman may be acquired as a wife in one of three ways, by *usus*, by written document, and by purchase. Although the Pentateuch records only the first means of acquiring a woman as a wife, the rabbis of the Talmud hold that the other two ways were also Biblically sanctioned by analogy from the Biblical verses. Maimonides accepted the first two ways as Biblical but rejected the third. He exercised his own method of analogy. He held that the marriage of women by *usus* was Biblical since it was written, "When a man has taken a woman and embraced her." The marriage by a written document he regarded as Biblical because the Bible said, "When a man wants to divorce his wife, then let him write a bill of divorcement," which implied that when the man married the woman, he had to write a bill of marriage. But the third method by purchase which he rejected as not being Biblical, he maintained had been introduced by the rabbis only by the analogy of words. The verb "take" was used in the Bible both in regards to marriage, as in the verse, "When a man had taken a woman" and in regard to a bill of sale as in the verse telling of Abraham's buying a piece of land from Ephron to bury his wife, Sarah. This analogy Maimonides rejected, as the words are not found in connection with the same subject matter. He, therefore, considered this method of marriage as purely rabbinical.[3]

According to the Talmudic law, it was not permissible to eat milk and meat together. This law was based on a verse in the Bible which forbids the seething of a kid in its mother's milk. This prohibition is repeated in the Pentateuch three times. The rabbis of the Talmud deduced from this injunction thrice repeated, three separate rules; one must not cook meat and milk together, but if one cooked them together, one must not eat thereof nor may one derive any benefit therefrom. The rabbis considered these three prohibitions Biblical. Maimonides accepted only the first two as such, but not the last. He regarded the prohibition of cooking milk and meat together as Biblical although the Bible lays down no specific injunction against doing so; the law on this subject was a matter of tradition given to the Jews by Moses, and accepted by Maimonides. He also accepted the Talmudic interpretation against eating of meat and milk together, as Biblical. He derived this prohibition against eating milk and meat together from a *kal vo-homer*—a minori ad majus.[4] Since the Bible prohibited cooking certainly eating was prohibited. He rejected the Talmudical prohibition of deriving benefit from meat and milk cooked together because the Bible does not forbid one from doing so nor can one derive such a prohibition by the method of *kal vo-homer*.

The same method, he applied in the laws of Impurity. In the Bible we read that any person who was under the same roof where a corpse was lying, was unclean for seven days. The Bible does not ascribe purity or impurity to a person who carries a dead body. The sages, however, maintained that if a person carries a corpse, he likewise is unclean for seven days and they included this among the Biblical laws. Maimonides accepted this by the argument of a *kal va-homer*, since, if a person who was under one roof with a dead body was unclean for seven days, certainly if he carried him, he should be unclean for seven days.[5]

Maimonides occasionally clarified the Law by apt illustrations. For example, in explaining the legal opinion that he held, that one who indirectly causes damage is guilty no less than the one who actually did the damage, he gave the following case: A man places cushions on the ground so that his dishes which he is throwing out of the window should not be broken. In the meantime another man passes by and removes the cushions so that the dishes were broken. The man who removed the pillows, although he did not do the actual breaking himself, is liable for the damage. Another case Maimonides cites is the following: A man throws dishes not his own out of the window to the ground where cushions lay to protect them from being smashed. Someone passes by and removes the cushions. Both parties are liable for the damage, although neither of them did the actual breaking; their actions caused the damage.[6]

Maimonides held that only a man who does a positive damage, that is, actually destroys property, is liable for damages. If, however, he does not destroy the property, but only decreases its value, he has done a negative damage and is not liable. One more case may be cited: A man has spoiled wheat which cannot be said to be destroyed but which cannot be used; it has what the Talmud calls an invisible damage. Maimonides said

buyer gives a deposit saying, if I withdraw, I shall forfeit my deposit; and the seller says, if I withdraw I shall return you not only the amount of your deposit but an additional sum. If the buyer withdraws, he forfeits his deposit because he has already given it to the seller. But if the seller withdraws, he returns the original amount but cannot be charged with the additional sum he promised to pay, since he never delivered it to the buyer. Maimonides also calls the seller's terms an *asmachta* also because there was no delivery.[13]

Other decisions of Maimonides relate to property. If one abandons his right to any property, real or personal, it ceases to be private property and becomes *res nullius*, property which belongs to no one. Anyone who obtains possession of it acquires title to it and becomes its owner. Hence one who finds lost property on the highways or in any public place, becomes its owner for it is assumed that the person who lost it has abandoned his right to it.

If a person buys stolen property, he must return it to the owner. The owner, however, must repay the buyer the equivalent amount of money that he had paid to the thief and recover the loss from him. This law that the lawful owner should repay to the buyer what he had given to the thief for the property was laid down to encourage trade. The burden of the loss was not put upon the innocent purchaser since otherwise people would refuse to buy openly from men not known to be honest. In this respect Jewish law differs from the common law under which no one can acquire title to stolen goods and the innocent purchaser suffers if the rightful owner proves that the stolen property is his. However, if the buyer bought from a notorious thief, the owner cannot be compelled to pay back to the buyer his money. In such a case, the rule in regard to the encouragement of trade cannot be applied. The buyer, of course, may try to recover his loss from the thief. If the owner of stolen property is known to have resigned himself to his loss, he is considered to have relinquished his rights to the stolen property itself. But the innocent purchaser though he might keep the property itself, had to pay him for his loss. However, if a buyer bought from a notorious thief, he had to return the property to the previous owner without any compensation even if he had relinquished his rights to the property.[14]

If one borrows money and gives a pledge as security, he loses his pledge if he does not pay his debt, and the bailee becomes the owner of the pledge. When the bailor gives the pledge to the bailee as security, the bailee obtains immediate possession of the property; therefore, it is not, according to Maimonides, a case of *asmachta*.[15] If the bailee gives a pledge of security from which the bailor derives profit, this profit, according to Maimonides, is to be considered usury. This applies to real estate as well. When the borrower conveys a field as security, the fruits of the field which the creditor obtains are usury. A pledge may be given to the creditor as security only when it is not necessary for the livelihood of the bailor. If the bailee takes such objects as pledges for security, he must return them. If he loses

the murderer to death in emergency cases. Since accessories could not be put to death according to the Talmudic Law, he declared that under no circumstances should they be allowed to escape punishment. For if the State did not punish them and the court did not want to use special dispensation, they must at least be punished corporeally and imprisoned for a long term.[19]

Maimonides held that though a minor who stole property could not be punished, according to the Talmudic Law, he should nevertheless be corporeally punished for his crime as a preventive measure.[19a]

Sometimes he decided against precedent when the employee in the case was to be taken into consideration. Though it had been held by his teachers that a plaintiff could recover a claim of less than two *perutot* (pennies) by taking an oath where the defendant denied the claim, Maimonides held that in such cases the plaintiff should not recover unless the sum involved was two *perutot*, but if he was a laborer, he might by taking an oath recover from his employer who denied the claim, even one *peruta.*[20]

Sometimes in deciding the law contrary to the decisions of the Gaonim, he appealed to a common sense of justice. For example, in a case where a man borrowed money in the presence of witnesses with the understanding that he was to return it in the presence of witnesses, the Gaonim decided that if he had returned in the presence of witnesses but they left the country, he had to pay the debt again. Maimonides naturally held it was not fair to make him pay a second time. He was to be believed that he had paid the debt.[21] If money was loaned in the presence of witnesses on the condition that it should be returned in the presence of certain specified people, and the debtor returns it in the presence of others, the Gaonim also held that the creditor could demand payment again. Maimonides again held that such a double payment was unjust. Since the debtor did return the loan though not in the presence of the people whom the creditor specified when he advanced the money, he should not be charged with repayment of the same debt. Maimonides appealed to common sense and asked what could the debtor do if the original witnesses or specified individuals had died. How was he able to prevent men from dying or interfere with their leaving the country? Was he to put those who wished to travel in jail?

On some matters on which Maimonides differed with the Gaonim, he was in error. He believed that the year in which he compiled the section of the Mishne Torah dealing with the laws of the Sabbatical year to be a Sabbatical year. "This year," he said confidently, "which is 4936 A.M. (1176 C.E.) 1107, according to the era of the destruction of the Temple, is a Sabbatical year." According to the calculation of the Gaonim, he said, it would be a post-Sabbatical year. Maimonides was mistaken. The chronology of the Gaonim was correct. According to a Tannaitic source the Temple was destroyed in a post-Sabbatical year. Maimonides had accepted the Talmudic statement that the Temple was destroyed in the year 3829 A.M., i.e., 68-69 C.E., which was a Sabbatical year, when as a matter of fact the Temple was

Impurity. He said they were scriptural ordinances, the reasons for which no one could infer from his own knowledge. They were statues which we had to follow. Similarly, the laws of the Mikveh according to which a person washed himself by certain rites and became pure, were also ordinances of the Scriptures.[24a]

Maimonides completed the Mishne Torah when he was forty-five years of age. He did not write this book in regular sequence. He wrote various sections at different times—a procedure which is noticeable throughout this great work. He compiled the seventh book which deals with the laws of the Sabbatical years, in 1176, but he wrote the introduction in 1177.

Did Maimonides have any purpose in writing the Mishne Torah? Did he intend, as his contemporaries charged, to supplant the Talmud with his book? There seemed at first to be grounds for this charge in the fact that he did not mention the name of any of the Tannaim or Amoraim. Further, he had stated in his introduction that anyone familiar with the Pentateuch would, after reading his Mishne Torah, have a knowledge of all the Oral Laws without having recourse to any other book. The charge of his contemporaries has been maintained by some modern scholars. Maimonides himself refuted it in his epistle to Pinhas, the Dayyan of Alexandria. He asked him to state when and where he had ever said that all other books should be destroyed or burned except his own book. He had made it very clear in his introduction that he had compiled the book to lighten the labors of the ordinary man in studying the Talmud. For this reason, he set forth all the laws in simple, concise language. He did not mention the names of the Tannaim and Amoraim because he listed most of them in his introduction. Besides, his book was a compilation and not a commentary. The method of the compilation is to present the subject matter without any discussion, as Rabbi Judah had done in his compilation of the Mishna. The other method was one of interpretation where it was necessary to explain the difficult passages and to reconcile seeming contradictions. His own book was emphatically a compilation, not a commentary. Furthermore, Rabbi Judah in compiling his Mishna also did not mention the names of all the Tannaim, in many cases stating the law anonymously. Other Tannaim besides Rabbi Judah did not record the names of the sages from Moses to their own days.[25]

In his letter to Jonathan of Lunel, Maimonides again repeated that his sole purpose in compiling his book was to render it easy for students to study the law, so that they should not be discouraged by the complications of the Talmud and led astray by the various opinions therein.[25a]

In his letter to his beloved student, Joseph ben Judah ibn Aknin, he said that he wrote his book for the glorification of God and not of himself. He had commenced his book for his own practical use, so that in his old age he should not be compelled to search for the Halacha through the entire Talmud. In other words, he began writing the book as a digest for himself. Realizing in the midst of his labors that the Jews had no code, free from controversies and errors, he sought to make his work serve the whole nation as well as himself, and compiled the book as it is. He said that he was perfectly aware that many people would try to destroy his book out of spite and envy, but that he was conscious that others would appreciate his labors. He was gratified that a number of scholars in France who read only part of his book, had asked him to complete it. He was confident the day would come when envy would disappear and his brethren would recognize the value of his book and would be very anxious to read it.[26]

The charge that he compiled the Mishne Torah so as to dispense with the Talmud can not be sustained, since he mentioned it in many passages of his book. By doing so, he invited the scholars who read his book to consult the Talmud for reference or comparison. Furthermore, in the first book of the Mishne Torah, he laid particular stress upon continually studying the Gemara. From all this we see that he did not want to dispense with the Gemara.

However, his explanation as to why he did not mention the names of the Tannaim and Amoraim in the Mishne Torah was far from being satisfactory. Rabbi Judah, in the Mishna, at times gave the names of individual Tannaim and at times spoke in the name of the sages, but Maimonides never gave any names. It should also be remembered that Maimonides gave additional Halachot which had never been given before. What did he really mean when he said that one who studied the Torah and his book did not need to study any other book? Did he, according to an accepted theory, codify the law just as Rabbi Judah had done, one thousand years before him?[26a] Did he seek to compile his Mishne Torah after Rabbi Judah's code, the Mishna, as a model? The answer to these questions is apparent when we realize that he meant to place his book alongside the Torah and not alongside the Mishna. The reasons for this view are numerous. He devoted much space in his book to the laws which were obsolete in his own time. He allotted one-third of his book to the laws of the Temple, the laws of Purification, the laws of Judges and Kings, none of which had any place in Jewish life after the destruction of the Temple. He did not follow the method of Alfasi who on compiling the Halachot, gave only the laws which had a place in Jewish life after the destruction of the Temple and other no longer existing institutions. Again Maimonides can not be called a codifier, for a codifier does not add new laws for which he has no authority nor does he decide the law against sources. But Maimonides in many cases decided the law contrary to the decisions in the Gemara and in the works of the Gaonim. We realize, then, that the statement in his introductions that if one studies his book as well as the Torah, one would not need to study any other book meant that he believed that his work bore a resemblance to the Torah rather than to the Mishna.

What then, was the purpose of Maimonides in compiling the Mishne Torah? The answer to this question, as will appear, is connected with his conception of the Messianic Age. It is clear from the *Iggeret ha-Shmad*, and particularly, his *Iggeret Teman*, that he expected that the Messiah would shortly arrive. In the latter work, he had said that the persecutions of the Jews under Christian rule in France and Germany, and the persecutions in the countries under Moslem control, undoubtedly were the predicted Jewish agony before the advent of the Messiah. He also said that the Messianic Age would be nigh just when the power of the Christians and the Moslems was at its height and their kingdoms were spreading throughout the world.

That was precisely the situation when he worked on his Mishne Torah. The critical moment had arrived and he had no doubt that Messiah would soon come. He said that the prophets had foretold that this very age in which he and his contemporaries were living was that of the Messianic era. The prophet Daniel undoubtedly held that the Jewish redeemer would come when Ishmael would have its Kingdom after the rise of Mohammed. Similarly, Isaiah when he said, "and I saw a chariot of asses, and a chariot of camels" had prophesied that Messiah would arrive after Mohammed. The chariot of asses referred to Messiah as proved by Zechariah's words, "Behold thy King cometh unto thee . . . riding upon an ass." He would arrive after the coming of the "rider on a camel" who was Mohammed, the King of the Arabs. Maimonides concluded that the arrival of the Messiah would take place after the uniting of Christians and Mohammedans, that is, after they had met in Palestine.

Maimonides, it will be recalled, gave as the date of

the returning of prophecy to Israel, the year 4976 A.M., i.e., 1216 C.E., which he believed would be followed very shortly by the coming of the Messiah. That Maimonides really expected the Messiah to come soon may be seen from his interpretation of the passage in Ezekiel where the prophet described the different sacrifices. Maimonides said that these sacrifices referred to the days of consecration of the third Temple when King Messiah would appear.[27] He gave a different interpretation from that in the Talmud wherein the prophecy of Ezekiel is taken to refer to the second Temple, that built in the time of Ezra.[27a]

Maimonides, then, expected the return of the Jews to Palestine shortly. This view does not conflict with his rationalism. He was not a mystic. He did not represent the Messiah as a supernatural person. He expressed his views on this subject a number of times in his writings. He held that Messiah would be a mortal, a king, a descendant of the house of David, as a man wiser than Solomon, and as a prophet next in greatness to Moses.[28] The returning of the Jews to Palestine would not be a supernatural event as many believed it would be; such a return would be the aftermath of a victory by the King over those in possession of the Holy Land. Thus it would be possible for the Jews to return.

Since Maimonides expected the Messiah to arrive soon, he prepared a *Jewish Constitution* for the occasion. He wrote this Constitution on the model of the Torah and not on that of the Mishna. Since a constitution does not give the names of authorities, he did not mention the names of individual scholars, but referred to the Tannaim or Amoraim, or Gaonim only collectively. Since a constitution sets forth not only the laws but also the principles of government,[29] as the Bible for example does, his Mishne Torah presented the principles and administration of Jewish government under the elements of the law. In the first book, he gave the principles of Judaism, and in the other books he codified all the laws. As the Unity of God is expressed in the first of the ten commandments so is the Unity of God set forth at the beginning of the Mishne Torah.

That Maimonides wanted to have his book second to the Torah of Moses is evident from the title, Mishne Torah (The Second Torah). He divided his book into fourteen parts because fourteen is the numeral value of the word *Yad*, part of the phrase "*Yad Ha-Hazaka*" occurring in the last verse of the Pentateuch which read, "To the strong hand, the great vision which Moses had performed for the eyes of the entire Jewish People." He could have divided this book into thirteen or fifteen parts. In fact, the division into fourteen parts is somewhat forced as his books on Judgments and Judges could have been comprised in one book. He also illogically discussed prohibited marriage and prohibited foods in one book.

He wrote his Mishne Torah, then, not with the Mishna compiled by Rabbi Judah in mind, but rather with the Torah of Moses in view. The Mishna which had been compiled about one thousand years previously was not the work of one man but of an academy, and comprised all the laws which were in force among the Jews before the time of its redaction. The Mishne Torah comprised not only all the laws but also those in force for the thousand years preceding its composition.

The manner in which Maimonides deduced Halachot from the numerous sources which he had used, is worthy of notice. He tells us that once some students inquired of him the source of a law of Homicide he cited in his book. He replied to them, that his Halachot on this subject were undoubtedly in the tractate *Makkoth* or *Sanhedrin* where the laws of Homicide are treated. When the students retorted that they looked high and low in these tractates, in the Babylonian and Palestinian Talmuds, as well as in *Tosefta*, and could not find the source for such a law as he advanced, he then told them that most likely he had used a source in the Talmud *Gittin*. To his great astonishment, after searching through this tractate he could not find the source there either. He abandoned his search but later he recalled that the law as he stated it in his book was deduced from the tractate *Yebamot* where the subject of Homicide is only casually mentioned.[30]

The Mishne Torah is, undoubtedly, the greatest and most important work (in Halacha) which was produced by the Jews during their entire history in the Diaspora because it gave the Jews a Constitution for a future State. It is moreover written in a wonderful style, is arranged in a remarkably systematic manner and presents a compilation of the entire Jewish law. But its preeminent uniqueness resides in the fact that it was prepared as a Jewish Constitution for a future Jewish State.

The Mishne Torah was welcomed by most of the Jews of Egypt. However, some mediocre rabbis either out of envy or jealousy, or for other personal reasons, began finding fault with the book. Pinhas, Dayyan of Alexandria, did not appreciate this masterpiece of Maimonides and looked for faults. He was especially eager to know why Maimonides did not mention the name of the Tannaim and why he decided the Halachot himself; he was also apprehensive lest the students studying the book, forsake the Talmud altogether.[30] He found another cause for his animosity towards the author. He was incited to oppose Maimonides through the circumstance that a rival Dayyan of Alexandria by the name of Daniel was a great admirer of his. Pinhas also accused Maimonides of lack of observance of some Jewish customs. To this, Maimonides replied that he never suggested any change in a custom which was generally practiced.[30a]

Samuel ben Ali of Bagdad was another opponent of Maimonides. Samuel who was head of the Yeshiva in Bagdad, sought to have his Yeshiva as the central authority on Jewish Law, and thus to control Jewish affairs in the Orient. He had tried to usurp the position of the Exilarch of Babylon when Daniel, the Exilarch, died leaving no heir. Petahya in the account of his itinerary gives us a description of Samuel ben Ali's vanity and the splendor by which he was surrounded. While in his official chair, he had an entourage of sixty servants armed with sabers. He is described as a haughty man who would not acknowledge anyone as his equal, much less, as his superior.[31] He did not consider anyone who had not studied in Bagdad as an authority in the Talmud. Although Samuel was a Talmudist in his own way, he was a fundamentalist and also a believer in astrology. Maimonides, it will be recalled, had attacked astrology in his book. Naturally, the rationalistic teachings of Maimonides did not please him. Moreover, Maimonides assumed an independent attitude in his book, and had never asked any authorization from Samuel ben Ali, whose sole desire was that the authority in the Jewish law should be vested in the Yeshiva of which he was the head.

When Maimonides' work reached France, at that time the seat of Jewish scholarship, the rabbis received it with some acclamation, although not with entire approval of his method. They saw that the book was a product of one of the greatest Jewish scholars, that it was not the work of an ordinary rabbi. However, one French scholar, Abraham ben David of Pasquieres, was very much opposed to the book and wrote *Hassagot* (criticism) attacking it. In his criticism, David, or as he is known, RaBaD, was not always fair to the author. He assailed him for his theological views and frequently indulged in severe acrimonious language using such terms as "this is not true,"—"this is not exact,"—"this is a mistake,"—"this reason has no sense." In another place, he said, "it seems to me that he (Maimonides) came only to confuse the whole world."[32]

between two laws established on the basis of verbal similarities in the text), were not Biblical unless so specified by the sages. He laid down fourteen fundamentals (principles) by which one could recognize what law was Biblical and what was Rabbinical. He wrote this book in the Arabic language but in latter days, regretted that he had not written it in Hebrew.[35] It was translated into Hebrew in the first part of the thirteenth century. There have been three translations, one by Abraham ibn Hasdai, another by Moses ibn Tibbon, and one by Solomon ibn Ayyub of Beziers, France.[36]

IX

CONTROVERSY WITH SAMUEL BEN ALI

In 1183-4, Maimonides married the sister of Abul Maali, Secretary to one of the wives of Saladin.[1] He had a daughter who died in childhood, and a son, Abraham, who was born in the month of Sivan, 1186.[2] Abraham, who very early showed a keen mind and a desire to study, received his education from his father. Abul Maali married Maimonides' sister. Through his influence, apparently, Maimonides became the personal physician to the Vizier of Saladin, el Fadil, who was the most influential man in Egypt. Thus, we may assume that it was through el Fadil's favor that the prestige of Maimonides grew greater. Through the influence of Maimonides, the Jews were welcomed to return to Jerusalem three years after Saladin recaptured it from the Franks in 1187.

But in that year, Maimonides faced a dangerous situation that almost put his life in jeopardy. He was charged by Abul Arab ibn Moisha who just arrived in Egypt with having betrayed the Moslem religion.[3] Abul Arab ibn Moisha had formerly been friendly to Maimonides, having been instrumental in saving his life in 1165 in Fez, when he was accused of being a Jew. Abul Arab

hand, he praised Samuel ben Ali highly. He was very loyal to his teacher and, incidentally, later married his only daughter—herself a scholar. The adverse criticism of Maimonides by Zekarya deeply wounded Joseph ibn Aknin.

In a letter to his master, ibn Aknin complained bitterly against Zekarya. Maimonides replied to him not to grieve over the matter and that it was not worth while to dispute with Zekarya. Although he regarded himself a great man, in fact the only one in his generation, Zekarya was really ignorant. Nevertheless, Maimonides himself admitted that some of Zekarya's objections to his commentary were well founded and that he expected to be guided by them.[6]

Zekarya was, therefore, certainly not an ignoramus but a Talmudic student. Maimonides told Aknin that he had received a letter from Bagdad from Samuel ben Ali in which he praised Zekarya very highly. It was apparent then these two men mutually admired each other.[7]

The unfriendly relations between Zekarya and ibn Aknin were due to reasons other than the fact that each of them was loyal to a master, with a different conception of Judaism. Ibn Aknin's opposition to Zekarya's mission in Aleppo to collect money for the Yeshiva of Bagdad must also have been a factor, as well as Samuel ben Ali's assumption that he was the real spiritual leader of entire Syria. Ibn Aknin considered such claims as an invasion upon the rights of Egyptian Jewry whose spiritual leader was Maimonides. Aleppo, at this time, was part of the great Kingdom of Saladin.

In 1190, ibn Aknin left for Bagdad for the purpose of establishing a Yeshiva in which instruction would be given according to the method and teachings of his great master, Maimonides. It was his intention to found a rival school to that of Samuel ben Ali. He also received Maimonides' permission and encouragement to do this. The master advised him to make use of his own Mishne Torah and the Halachot of Alfasi as text books, and, in case of contradictions between these two books, to refer to the Talmud but not lose time on the discussions therein.[8] He thus advocated a different method of teaching from that prevailing in the Yeshiva of Samuel ben Ali. He warned Aknin that the establishment of the Yeshiva would place great responsibility upon him and interfere with his business. He advised him never to take any emoluments, not even a penny from the community. It was much better to earn one *drahme* by a trade, such as tailoring or carpentry, than to receive compensation from the Exilarch. He recommended Aknin to continue his own business and also not to abandon the study of medicine.[9]

After ibn Aknin arrived in Bagdad or possibly shortly before, Samuel the Rosh Gelutha (Exilarch) died. Samuel ben Ali opposed the appointment of the newly suggested Exilarch, on the ground that he was not scholarly enough. In reality, he was not in favor of having an Exilarch at all.

When back in 1174-5 the Exilarch Daniel died, without issue, Samuel ben Ali had opposed the appointment of a new Exilarch, but he had to yield to the pressure of public opinion. Samuel of the family of Joshiah, the son of Zakkai, at that time became Exilarch. Now, with the death of the Exilarch, Samuel ben Ali aagin tried to abolish the office. He considered himself the successor of the great teachers of the two schools of Sura and Pumbeditha. He even claimed descent from the prophet Samuel.[10] He maintained that the Jews in the Diaspora ought not to have a ruler like that of a King and that they needed instead a scholar to guide them and explain the precepts and their religion. He disapproved of collecting taxes from the Jews by the Exilarch as interfering with the rights of the Yeshiva, the seat of the Torah.

In his letters to the community of Damascus, Samuel ben Ali also maintained that the heads of the Yeshivot, the Gaonim, had the right to ordain scholars in the Diaspora. Claiming this authority by such precedent, he ordained Zekarya.

Maimonides was opposed to Samuel ben Ali's views and especially his desire to abolish the office of the Exilarch. In his Mishne Torah he had written that the Exilarchs in Babylon occupied the position of the ancient place of the Kings. They ruled the Jewish communities with or even without their consent and they had the authority to appoint judges. Apparently the opposition of Samuel ben Ali to Maimonides was not based alone on the merits of the Mishne Torah or his disagreement with decisions therein but rather on the fact that Maimonides and his pupil, ibn Aknin who was then in

Bagdad to carry out his master's views, were responsible for thwarting his life's ambition to abolish the Exilarchate and to proclaim himself the sole leader of the Babylonian Jews.

Samuel ben Ali and Maimonides thus entertained different conceptions of Judaism. Samuel ben Ali maintained that the leadership of the Jews should be vested in a man of spiritual authority, like the Gaon, while Maimonides held that it should be vested in the Exilarch, the political leader. In this Maimonides proved himself a pioneer of Jewish nationalism.

The new Exilarch, who had been appointed in spite of ben Ali's opposition, sent a letter to Maimonides in Egypt, in which he apparently sought his endorsement of his appointment, for Maimonides' prestige was great. This letter was read publicly in Maimonides' home on the festival of Tabernacles by Samuel the Melamed (teacher) in the presence of the leaders of the entire Jewish community. The reading of this letter, and the fact that the leaders of the Jewish community of Egypt stood as it was read, was a token of the recognition accorded by them to the Exilarch. On hearing this, Samuel ben Ali, in a letter to Maimonides dated Sivan, 1191, criticized the appointment of the new Exilarch on the ground that he did not possess sufficient scholarship, and he declared that Maimonides had no right to endorse him.

In Heshvan, 1191, a few months after Maimonides had written to his pupil, ibn Aknin in answer to his complaint that Samuel ben Ali had abused him verbally and in writing, Maimonides advised him to disregard Samuel's abuse and not to misjudge him. "Who would not cry out if he were wounded?" Maimonides asked. Naturally ben Ali was hostile because Aknin was in favor of the Exilarchate. Had it not been for his opposition, Samuel ben Ali would have crushed the Exilarchate. Maimonides told Aknin to remember that, after all, he was much younger than Samuel and that it was not advisable to quarrel with one advanced in age who was respected as the head of a Yeshiva. He advised him to be patient and submissive instead. It was to be regretted, of course, that many people, particularly those who attain power like Samuel, become very haughty. Maimonides said that he had already complied with Aknin's request to write to the Exilarch. He also told Aknin to say to Samuel ben Ali that he himself had been involuntarily dragged into this controversy in Bagdad; yet he would not retract anything he had said; what he had done—was done. Maimonides, also, informed Aknin that he had forwarded him the first part of his new book, the *Moreh Nebuchim* and that he was now sending him the Introduction.[11]

In this letter, Maimonides gives us a personal account of his own labors. He said that he had secured the post of physician to el Fadil as well as to Kadhi al-Kodhah (Supreme Judge). These positions, however, were not very remunerative. He still pursued his private practise which was so extensive that when he returned to Fostat, he was greatly exhausted. He was so much occupied that it was very difficult for him to pursue research in medicine, and he could study the Torah on the Sabbath only. He found no time to glance at scientific books. He had just received the books ibn Roshd (Averroes) had compiled on the works of Aristotle, but was only able to make a cursory examination of them which had convinced him that Averroes was practically correct in his method.

Maimonides also mentioned the death of his little daughter but consoled himself that God knew His ways. In sending him greetings, he did not include Aknin's wife, Sarah, for it was against the Jewish law to inquire about a married woman, but he told him that he was praying for his wife, as well as for him. "May you have peace and may your house (wife) have peace. A year from hence Sarah will have a son."

A reference in this letter to an adjustment of accounts that was to be made by Aknin with ibn al Moshat, when the latter returned from India, is of great interest. It leads one to suppose that Maimonides, after his brother was drowned at sea, continued his jewelry business. Apparently ibn al Moshat was the actual business man, while Maimonides and his pupil ibn Aknin, were his partners.

This letter was written by Maimonides in the Fall of 1191,[12] and in it he made reference to a letter he had received from Yemen questioning him about his views on Resurrection. He states that he had answered it, but that he intended later to write a treatise on the subject. In this allusion to the matter of Resurrection, we arrive at the controversy between Maimonides and Samuel ben Ali.

Samuel ben Ali, who considered himself the greatest Talmudist of his time, saw in Maimonides a serious rival in scholarship. He feared that his prestige was in danger of being eclipsed, and sensed a menace to his determined ambition to abolish the Exilarchate. He sought an opportunity to show to the Jewish world that he was not only as great a scholar and scientist as Maimonides, but was even greater. He determined to prove that Maimonides' theological points of view were not well taken. The opportunity soon presented itself to him in the controversy about Resurrection which at that time broke out and in which Maimonides ultimately became involved.

Shortly after the Mishne Torah was written, some students in Damascus quoted it in defense of their stand against the doctrine of Resurrection. In the year 1189, some Yemenite Jews wrote to Maimonides personally questioning him on his belief in Resurrection, and asking him in particular whether he held that the body would be completely annihilated and the soul never be united with it after death. They also wanted to know whether reward and punishment referred to the soul only and not to the body as well. Maimonides sent a letter in reply. The Yemenite Jews forwarded a copy of it to Bagdad, to Samuel ben Ali, together with the original queries. Samuel ben Ali then wrote a special epistle on the subject in which he declared that Maimonides was utterly mistaken in his views.

In 1191, some of Maimonides' friends in Babylonia wrote to him informing him what the Yemenite Jews had done and at the same time they sent him Samuel ben Ali's epistle criticising his views. Maimonides was now compelled to write a treatise on Resurrection[13] and he finished it in the same year. In it he said that he would make no additional statements to what he had already written in the commentary on the Mishna and the Mishne Torah. He regretted that he would have to repeat many matters at length so that women and ignoramuses would understand. It is apparent that he was very much irritated.

He protested against those who charged him with saying that the passages in the Bible referring to Resurrection were to be interpreted allegorically. He defied anyone to point out where he had said this. He had only said that the question of Ezekiel's revival of the dead, discussed in the Talmud, was a controversial one. In a controversial matter there was no final conclusion and one could side with either of the partisans. He himself held that Resurrection was not in accordance with nature, and he believed in it only as a miracle. He did not deny that the Talmud contained passages in which it was declared that those who would be resurrected would continue to enjoy their earthly pleasures. His own theory was that those resurrected would live again for a very long period in the Messianic Age where long life would be the rule. But, after having lived a long life they would die again to find eternal life only

ing Samuel for praising him and for the defense on his behalf to the Jews of Yemen. He said that he was always glad to answer criticism upon his work and was ready to accept any correct suggestions. He had the greatest respect for Samuel ben Ali because of his position and scholarship. He was perfectly aware that the laws concerning Sabbath limits were Biblical enactments. Samuel had attributed to him false views; not from lack of comprehension but because of a hasty consideration of Maimonides' writings. As a matter of fact, he had included in his Book of Precepts which dealt only with Biblical enactments, the laws of Sabbath limits. If ben Ali had more carefully studied the Mishne Torah, where the Laws of Sabbath were dealt with, he would have found more detailed consideration of the laws concerning the Sabbath limits.

The responsum to Abraham ha-Kohen of Bagdad took up only the question whether the laws of Sabbatical limits were Rabbinical or Biblical in respect to travelling on water. He had decided that here they were Rabbinical. It was permissible to travel on the Sabbath on the rivers Tigris and Euphrates, as well as on the Nile because they were wide and deep just as it was permissible to travel on the high seas. The fact that the rivers were fresh water and the sea salt water made no difference in respect to travel on the Sabbath. That some of the Gaonim had prohibited travelling on rivers on the Sabbath made no difference. Perhaps they believed that there was a distinction between travelling on the sea because it was salty and on a river because it was fresh water. As long as we did not know the reasons for their enactments, we cannot accept their decisions as final. It is well known that many scholars travelled on the Sabbath on rivers which were as wide and as deep as the Tigris and Euphrates.[15]

The opponents of Maimonides did not cease their attacks upon him after his reply to Samuel ben Ali's strictures. They also sought to discredit him on the ground that he was neither a Talmudist nor a truly religious man. There arose on the other hand admirers who defended him from these charges. But an opportunity came to him to exonerate himself from these groundless accusations. A man named Joseph ibn Gabir,[16] who did not know Hebrew, sought to defend him from various attacks made on the Mishne Torah. He asked him to translate the Mishne Torah into the Arabic language so that he might read it, and write a defense in his behalf. Maimonides replied that he was thankful to him for his good intentions but that he would not translate his book into Arabic. He was on the contrary more anxious to have his works originally written in Arabic (the Commentary on the Mishna and the Book of Precepts) translated into Hebrew. He advised him to study Hebrew so as to be able to read the Mishne Torah; nor would this be difficult as it was written in very simple style. He told him not to be discouraged from studying Hebrew because of his age. Others had taken it up later in life, had become great sages, and were cited in the Talmud.

He then entered upon what is virtually an *apologia*

X

THE GUIDE TO THE PERPLEXED

ABOUT the year 1190, Maimonides finished his second great work, *Dalalat al-Hairin, Moreh Nebuchim,* the Guide to the Perplexed.[1] Like his Commentary on the Mishna, it was written in the Arabic language but with Hebrew characters. It was intended as a guide not only for his disciple, Joseph ibn Aknin, but for perplexed thinkers whose studies brought them into conflict with religion, and for students of philosophy bewildered by the ambiguous and figurative expressions employed in the Scriptures.

Maimonides said in the Introduction, which was in the form of a letter to Aknin, that upon receiving his early letters from Alexandria he had formed a high opinion of him. His estimate of him rose still higher when he observed the acumen Aknin showed when he studied under him. Now that Aknin had left Egypt, his absence had prompted him to compose this work. He had promised to send to him each chapter as soon as it was completed.

The *Moreh Nebuchim* was divided into three parts, besides the Introduction. In the first part, Maimonides dealt with the interpretations of Biblical anthropomorphism. He said that some of the anthropomorphic words used were homonymous, that is, had other meanings. Other words were imperfectly homonymous, and employed in some instances only figuratively. He dealt with the different divine attributes which should not be applied directly or indirectly, to God.[2]

Maimonides also dealt with *Kalam* (Mohammedan Theology), the method of which, he believed was taken from the Christian fathers who had applied it in the defense of their religious doctrines. Some of the Jews, particularly those in the East and in Africa, had also adopted the method of the Kalam. In doing so, they followed the *Mútazilah School* (Dissenting Mohammedans) not because this school was superior to the *Ashariya* School (Orthodox Mohammedans) but because at the time the Jews became acquainted with the *Kalam*, it was studied only in the *Mútazilah* School. The Jews in Spain, however, followed the Aristotelian philosophy.

In the second part, he proved the existence of one Creator, a Primal Cause, who was absolutely incorporeal, and without resemblance or relation whatsoever to anything else. He also treated of the intelligences of the spheres which he identified with the angels mentioned in the Bible. He discussed the theory of *Creatio ex-Nihilo* which he accepted. He gave a discourse upon the *Maaseh Bereshit*, The Account of the Creation. He also dealt at length with the problem of prophecy, to which we shall later refer.

In part three, he entered with great caution upon

bid the doing of certain things that are associated with idolatry. It was forbidden to shave the beard and the earlocks because it was the custom of heathen priests to do this.[3] Similarly, one was not allowed to wear garments made of linen and wool as heathen priests wore such a mixed cloth.[4] The precepts that women should not wear men's garments and vice-versa, were given with the vestures of these priests in mind. Maimonides, however, found another reason for this precept, namely, that the interchange of dress creates lust and leads to immorality.[5]

The third class contains the precepts which relate to moral conduct. The reason for these precepts, he says, is distinctly clear in their object namely to teach ethical principles.

In the fourth class, Maimonides includes the precepts relating to Charity, Loans, Gifts and the like. The value of these precepts is apparent. They teach one to have sympathy with the poor and to assist them in various ways without wounding their feelings. They also teach one not to trouble those who are helpless. Maimonides explains why the first fruits should be given to God. By doing so, man accustoms himself to be generous, to limit his appetite and to curb his desire for wealth.

The reciting of the portion of the Law when one brings the first fruits to the Temple tends also to create humility. This ceremony teaches man that it is essential in the service of God to remember former troubles and past distress, during days of wealth and comfort.

The precepts concerning the year of release and the Jubilee year, promote the well being of mankind. They also enable the land to become more fertile and increase its produce through remaining fallow for an interval of time. The precepts concerning the care and freeing of slaves are very evident. This may also be said of the rules which prescribe acts of mercy and kindness to the poor. All these precepts make mankind realize that fortune is unstable, that he who is rich today may some day be poor himself, or that his descendants may suffer poverty.

The fifth class contains those precepts which relate to the prevention of wrong and violence and to the committing of injuries and damages. The purpose of these precepts is to provide for punishing the offenders. He also explains the purpose of the law that one who unintentionally kills another must go into exile and remain there until the death of the High Priest. It is to keep him in "protective custody." "The avenger of the blood" will become more reconciled since the cause of his trouble is gone. The death of the High Priest as the time limit of exile is made so that the relatives of the slain person will become resigned to their own loss. Among the Jews, the death of no person was more bitterly bewailed than that of the High Priest.[6]

The sixth class contains the laws of Theft, Robbery and False Witnesses. Maimonides explains why he who steals sheep must pay double the value instead of their

Such prayers formally educate man in the love of God, and teach him the right belief concerning Him.

The tenth class contains the laws bearing upon the Temple, Ministers of the Temple and the Sacrifices. Maimonides gives the reason why Abraham selected Mount Moriah as a place for the future Temple. Since idolaters used to select high mountains on which to build their temples and place their images, Abraham proclaimed the Unity of God from a high mountain. He selected the west as the place for worship because he did not wish to follow the idolaters who worshipped the Sun as a deity and turned their faces to the east.[9] He adopted the reverse process and chose the west, turning his back towards the Sun. As it is said, "The Shekinah is in the West."[10] Sacrifices were permitted the Jews as a compromise. Since before the coming of Moses they had, like the other nations among whom they lived, been accustomed to sacrifice animals in the temples, and since they would have found it very difficult to discontinue these methods of worship, God allowed them to continue to sacrifice animals. He, however, transferred the sacrifices which were offered to the images to His own service.[11] He also restricted them to one place, the Temple and to one group, the Priesthood. The sacrificial service is not the primary object of service to God; prayer and reading the Torah are more important. Thus Jews were allowed to bring only the animals for sacrifice but not to slaughter them themselves. Sacrifices were restricted and kept within bounds but prayers may be offered anywhere and by anybody.

In order to arouse great reverence for the Temple and those who minister therein, special honors were rendered the latter. The priests were ordered to be clad in beautiful garments. Those who had blemishes or presented an abnormal appearance were excluded from the service since the masses judge a man by his outward appearance. The Levites did not take part in the sacrifice; their duty consisted in singing hymns so as to arouse religious emotions.

Incense was burned twice daily in the Temple to produce a pleasant odor. So many animals were slaughtered in the Temple that the atmosphere would have been as malodorous as that of a slaughter house. The anointing of oil marked the anointed objects or persons with distinction and surrounded them with fragrance. In this respect a garment or a vessel was put on the same plane as a human being.[12]

The eleventh class sets forth the laws commanding certain special sacrifices. These precepts were intended to eradicate false ideas entertained by heathens, like the Egyptians, who worshipping Aries abstained from killing sheep, or like the Sabean[13] sect who worshipped demons which they thought assumed the form of goats. The Jews were purposely ordered to sacrifice sheep and goats since they symbolized heathen Gods. The act of slaughtering them, considered by the heathen as a heinous crime, was made a means of approaching God by the Jews.

Maimonides offers an explanation why the sacrifice of a sin offering was to be made not on the altar but outside of the camp and why the scapegoat of the Day of Atonement was to be slaughtered in the wilderness. Sin was thus symbolically removed as far as possible and no trace of it left for the sacrifice was entirely destroyed by fire. Maimonides admitted that sin could not be removed from a person and transferred to an animal, but he says that the sacrifices and ceremonies by which this was manifestly done were of a symbolic character to impress man and induce him to repent.

The twelfth class deals with the precepts of Cleanness and Uncleanness. Their general purpose was to prevent people from entering the Temple too often so that the infrequency of their visits will make them approach it with greater reverence and be more highly impressed with its splendor.

The thirteenth class includes the Dietary laws; prohibiting certain foods because they are unwholesome. Pork, for instance, contains too much moisture, is indigestible, and is the product of the swine, an animal with filthy habits, whose food is putrid and loathsome. Incidentally, the prohibition against eating pork by rendering the raising of swine unnecessary makes for sanitary surroundings. The fat of the intestines is forbidden since it produces indigestion and constipation.[14] Meat and milk cooked together produce heavy food. Maimonides thinks it likely that the heathens used milk with meat on some of their festivals. The prohibition therefore sought to abolish any vestige that savoured of idolatry. He also offers an explanation of the Biblical injunction against eating fish which has no fins or scales. His theory is that the fins or scales in themselves have no bearing on this prohibition, but are really means of determining the quality of the fish for food.

The fourteenth class contains the precepts of Forbidden Marriage, and the laws of Circumcision. Prostitution was prohibited by the law not only because it was immoral but because children born of a prostitute would not know their father and be ostracized and unhappy. Another important reason for forbidding prostitution was to restrain excessive and continual sensuality. Lust is formed by variety of indulgence. A different woman arouses more ardent sexual desire than the same woman to whom one has become accustomed for a long time.

The reason why a Jew is not allowed to marry a bastard is not so much to punish the bastard as to prevent illicit relations. People will be more cautious about entering into such relations when they realize that their children will be outcasts in society unable to marry. The laws against incestuous relations and marriages within the proper degrees of blood relationship are given partly to teach a man not to overestimate sexual intercourse and not to desire it often. Capital punishment is inflicted upon those guilty of incestuous intercourse or forbidden marriages. Such a preventive measure was necessary to restrain the people from entering into connections for which there is a great temptation and more than usual facilities since blood relations are constantly together in the same house. The law compels the man who seduced a girl to marry her because he is obviously the fittest husband for her; he can heal her sorrow and redeem her character better than any one else.

Circumcision is prescribed for the purpose of limiting sexual desire so as to weaken the organ of generation as much as possible.[15] Circumcision becomes, also, a bodily sign distinguishing all the members of the same faith.[16]

Maimonides endeavored to find a rational basis for all the commandments and prohibitions, even for the *Hukkim* (statutes) some of which he believed served as a protection against idolatry.

The punishments for the transgression of the precepts and laws vary, some being severe and others lenient, depending on different conditions. Severity must be exercised when the crimes cause great injury, when they are frequently committed, and when great temptation exists to commit them. Prohibitions, which a person may violate secretly, must also be severely punished to deter him.

Some of Maimonides' explanations of the laws were anticipated by the sages of the Talmud and Midrash. The reason he assigns for the institution of sacrifice is found in the Midrash. However, some of his explanations of the reasons for the precepts, are contrary to the opinions held by the sages. His theories about the origin of the precepts are in many instances forced and are not historically correct. To trace the origin of the different precepts, one must not only be familiar with the early history of the Jewish people, but must also have a knowledge of the history of comparative religion. In these, Maimonides was lacking. Although he made a study of the entire literature dealing with idolatry, that alone was not sufficient. First, he obtained his information from books that were more or less contemporary, and secondly, he did not have a historical conception of the development of religion. Of course, he lived in the twelfth century when philosophy of history was not known. He even sought and believed he found reasons for the different *Hukkim* (statutes), which being decrees of law can not be explained, as the Talmud says.[17] It is most likely that the *Hukkim* which are found in the Torah are traceable to Moses' hostility to the common customs and laws which prevailed at that time among the different tribes or nations. It is of some interest to note that when the Torah used the word *Hukkim*, it is connected with the word "walk." "You should not walk in the *Hukkim* (statutes) of the gentiles." The term *Halacha*, which was used by the early Tannaim is derived from the word "*Holach*" walk, and refers in the early Tannaitic literature to common law and early customs.[18]

Maimonides in his book, *Moreh Nebuchim*, as well as in his Commentary on the Mishna, tried to prove his views on philosophy and psychology by citing various verses in the Bible into which he unconsciously read his ideas. In doing so, he followed the method of the sages who tried to read into the Bible their Halakic point of view. This attempt to derive various ideas of theology and ethics from the Bible is apparent through-being was never perfect. Law was divinely given, it was to be universally applied, and was to be followed irrespective of times or places. It was not like medicine, the administering of which depended upon varying conditions, persons and times.[23]

The view that certain laws no longer have a *raison d'etre* and need not be observed, was a mistaken one. Furthermore, the Jewish law must not be abrogated, because the chain of Jewish history might be broken. Maimonides observed even the customs to which he was opposed, since they were observed by the Jews for many generations;[24] he followed the tradition so as not to destroy the unity of the Jewish people. However, he did not engage in the practises which were based on superstitions or some tenet to which Judaism was opposed. The precepts would be abolished only when the Jewish people as a whole reached perfection, that is in the *Olam Haba* (The Future World). It would not be necessary to observe the commandments and precepts there.[25] The righteous would sit with crowns on their heads and enjoy the Divine Glory.

Maimonides wrote to his pupil, Joseph ibn Aknin, that he would be satisfied if by his *Moreh Nebuchim*, he removed the doubts of a reader even on one perplexing problem. If a reader derived no benefit whatsoever from the book, he may then consider the work as never having been written and so the author failed in his purpose. Of course, he wrote his book for intelligent people but even then he had hesitated before writing on the *Maaseh Bereshit* (theology) and the *Maaseh Mercabah* (metaphysics) since they were profound mysteries. No Jewish scholars since the time of the Jewish captivity had written about them.[26]

In the letter to ibn Aknin in which he told him that he was sending him the Introduction of the Moreh, he asked him not to let the Arabs know of the book for fear they would injure the author. He had given his book for the purpose of copying it to only one man, the pious judge Abul Machasen.[27] Maimonides feared he would incur the wrath of the Arabs for what he had written about Prophecy and about Mohammed whom he charged with taking some of his doctrines from Moses. However, the book was soon transcribed into Arabic letters and was read by the Arabs. Far from persecuting him for the book, they praised it very highly. They declared that everything that he wrote was correct except his views on Prophecy.[28]

The work was translated into Hebrew by Samuel ibn Tibbon during the lifetime of Maimonides, and later by Jehudah Al Harizi. It was translated into Latin in the thirteenth century,[29] and into Italian in the latter part of the sixteenth century. It also appeared in other living languages. Many commentaries have been written on the Moreh Nebuchim, the most outstanding ones being by Moses Narboni, Shem-tob, Profiat Duran (Efodi), Crescas and Isaac Abarbanel.

the spread of the study of the Torah. He held, furthermore, that a man who studies should be exempt from all civic duties and not be compelled to take part in public affairs. Only they who had already completed their studies should take part in communal matters. He therefore would exclude a student from the "ten men of leisure" who, in every community, were supposed to be "minute men" ready to serve the public interest, communal or religious.[5]

Maimonides devised a parable in which he divided Humanity into six categories, and compared them to six groups of subjects in relation to their King.[6] In the parable set forth, he represented the King in his palace, and placed one group of his subjects in foreign lands. Each of the remaining five groups in the King's domain was depicted as taking a different stand with respect to the palace itself. The members of one turned their backs upon it. Another group was eager to enter but had not yet caught a glimpse of it. A third group reached it and searched for the entrance gate. Those in the fourth class passed through the gate, and walked into the ante-chamber, while the fifth group entered the inner palace where the King resided but did not converse with him.

Maimonides compared those in the first category of Humanity to the subjects who stayed away from their own country. Those in this category were without religion and were really not to be regarded as complete human beings; they were below the level of men and only higher than apes. The second category was like those in the group who had their backs turned towards the palace; it had religion and intelligence but held doctrines, whose falsity made them recede further from the Supreme King. Those who constituted this category were in a worse position than those in the first category. Under certain circumstances it might be necessary to slay them and thus exterminate their doctrine in order that they should not mislead others.

Although Maimonides was very liberal in respect to other religions, he followed the Torah which laid down the doctrine that a Jew who beguiles his fellow Jew from God shall be put to death. Saladin who also was tolerant to other religions, such as Christianity and Judaism, but would not tolerate heresy or schism in his own religion, Islam, maintained a similar attitude towards heretics. Thomas Aquinas, who was more severe, held that a heretic should always be put to death. He justified the death penalty on the theory that the heretic, who falsifies true religion, is a worse offender than the counterfeiter who debases the coin of the realm. Since the counterfeiter is punished by death, surely the heretic should be likewise punished.[7]

One must remember of course, that Maimonides was in many respects the child of his own age and like his Moslem and Christian contemporaries believed that the heretic was a dangerous enemy of the State. He regarded the Jewish heretic as a menace because he threatened the existence of a people who had no country of their own and whose religion took the place of the State. Yet he was more liberal than his age when he said that only under certain circumstances the heretic must be exterminated.

The third category of Humanity resembling the subjects who wanted to reach the palace but had never yet seen it, was made up of the masses who observed the divine commandments but were ignorant. The fourth category, comparable to those who had reached the palace searching for the entrance gate, devoted themselves to the study of the Law, believed in the true principles of faith, and worshipped God, but were not trained in philosophical treatment of the principles of the Law. The fifth category resembling those who entered the ante-chamber was made up of those who studied the principles of religion. The sixth category constituted all who had mastered metaphysics and succeeded in finding a proof for everything that could be proven; they had a true knowledge of God so far as true knowledge could be obtained. They had reached the goal and were like the subjects in the palace in which the King lived.

In his classification, Maimonides placed one who studies the science of the principles of religion higher than him who observes the divine commandments. He shocked some of the rabbis who heard this view; they refused to believe that he really entertained it. They declared, however, that if he put it in writing, the part of the book containing the passage should be burned.[8]

Yet there is nothing startling in this passage. Maimonides always held that study of the commandments came first and was of greater value than actual observance of them, because knowledge leads to observance but observance does not lead to knowledge.[9]

His conception of human relations was influenced both by Rabbinical Judaism and Aristotelian philosophy. His general views of life may be briefly summarized. Man should not pass from one extreme to another in his behavior. He should not be prodigal or penurious —he should always observe the middle path, what Aristotle calls "the mean." He should neither excessively indulge in physical enjoyment nor practise asceticism. He should not be like monks who remain celibate nor like hermits who eat no meat and drink no wine, and who wander in the wilderness clothed in hairy garments and sack cloth. Maimonides did not deny that some pious Jews in former days had been ascetic and renounced marriage, foregone eating meat, and dwelt in the mountains and wilderness. He found extenuating circumstances in their case. They either sought spiritual perfection or feared they would be contaminated by association with the wicked and become corrupt in their own morals.

But society in general cannot act like the hermit. It cannot imitate the ascetic acts of the pious man, for not having his motives it would only destroy itself. Those who imitate saints may be compared to laymen who have no knowledge of medicine. A physician sometimes prescribes medicine which has poisonous ingredients. It would be foolhardy to assume that a healthy person would be improved by this same medicine. As a matter of fact, by taking it he might make himself sick and

advised the Jews rather to hire employees than own slaves.[18]

In litigation between employer and employee, Maimonides usually favored the employee. While a master might not assign his slave humiliating work, the employer could demand performance of the work for which he hired an employee. He considered an employee a free agent. The employee being free can choose his work. If he agreed to perform menial labors, he is bound to carry out his agreement.[19] Reference was made previously to the case which involved only one penny, where the employee was permitted to recover his claim upon taking an oath. The court administered the oath and heartened him with such an introductory remark as, "Don't grieve—swear and you will get the money."[20]

Another provision favoring the employer was, not allowing a night worker to engage in day work also, for he might not be in efficient condition to carry out his duties to his day time employer.[21]

Employees could not be discharged without warning (notice). But incapable public employees, such as incompetent teachers or careless secretaries who dated documents wrongly or who otherwise proved inefficient, could be dismissed without such notice.[22]

Maimonides, on the other hand, would not allow the employee to take advantage of the employer. He must conscientiously perform his duties while he is working.

Man is a social being and seeks to be a member of society.[23] Hence, Maimonides believed that people should associate only with scholars and virtuous people, for by associating with the ignorant or wicked they might be contaminated and adopt their ways and habits. Men should also observe the customs of the society in which they live. They should not be arrogant and hold themselves aloof from their fellow creatures.[24]

Maimonides, like the sages of old, believed that every man should have a trade by which he could support himself. His duty was then to marry. Maimonides disapproved of a man's marrying before he had a trade by which to support his wife.[25] He considered the family the foundation of the State.[26] Capital punishment was fixed by law as the sentence for those who cursed their parents because they undermined the foundation of the family and hence the State. Maimonides justified the husband's right to render void the vows taken by his wife, because they might cause friction in the family.

Maimonides thought that the marriage between relatives made for greater happiness as they were congenial to one another. Provided the limits of blood relationship were not overstepped, the closer the relation, the better. He was in favor of a man's marrying his niece, the daughter of his brother or sister.[27]

The authority of the State was to be supreme. It could demand obedience to the laws, and levy taxes. It could properly confiscate the property of one who tried to defraud the government. Confiscated property could be legally sold at auction and its former owner could not claim its return to him from the purchaser. Maimonides considered any act, even of a dictator, legal as long as it

races or nations.[31] But, if anyone wanted to embrace the Jewish religion, he was made welcome. Although his forefathers were heathens, he could, like the rest of the Jews, invoke their God in the prayers which read: "God, our God, and the God of our fathers."[32] Maimonides thus demonstrated that, although the Jewish religion was accepted only by the Jews, it need not be confined to them alone or to Semites in general. Anyone who became a proselyte was entitled to all the privileges of a Jew.

He did not consider Islam an idolatrous religion nor the Mosque a house of idolatry.[33] He did regard the Christians as idolators because while in Palestine, he saw the Crusaders with their ikons, and he thought they worshipped them as idols. He, therefore, forbade the Jews to have commercial intercourse with Christians during the days of their festivals.[34] His misapprehension was due to the fact that he was scarcely acquainted with Christians and was not familiar with their religion. However, Maimonides knew that the Christians recognized the Bible as of divine authority and, therefore, he held that a Jew might teach the Bible to Christians but not to Moslems, since they denied its divine inspiration.[35]

He displayed the same liberal attitude to Karaites that he did to other religions. He did not consider them heretics. He did not abuse them, for they had no choice when born and should not be charged for the schism introduced by their forefathers.[36] Jews ought always to be liberal to them, help them, mingle in their society, and thus prepare them for a return to Judaism. However, he sought to ward off any influence of the Karaites upon the Jews, and he held that any Jew who obeyed their laws should be punished.

Maimonides, it must be emphasized, was essentially a rationalist. He placed reason above all other human faculties. He regarded superstition as a species of idolatry. He was opposed to belief in omens which he also considered idolatry. A man who regarded the falling of his cane on the floor, or some other insignificant happening as an omen that he should not leave the house and who consequently stayed at home, was really practising idolatry. He did not even approve of Eliezer's manner of choosing a wife fit for Isaac when he determined to take the girl who offered a drink to his camels as well as to him. Maimonides interpreted Eliezer's resolve in the nature of waiting for an omen.[37]

The use of amulets, quite often mentioned in the Talmud, he considered a superstition and he, therefore, never mentioned them in his Mishne Torah.

He differed with some of the Talmudists who held that the Mezuzah was put on the door posts to guard the family. He believed that its service consisted in reminding one, on leaving the house, to think of God, and thus not to harbor wicked thoughts or to commit evil deeds. He maintained that anyone who inscribed the names of angels in the Mezuzah would not have any portion in the *Olam Haba.*[38]

He considered the pursuit of astrology almost as reprehensible as the practise of witchcraft. The fate of man was not interlinked with constellations. His acts depended upon himself and not upon destiny. Man could choose his own career and become a scholar or a saint. One's acts did not hinge upon the stars. Only ignoramuses believed that a person born under a particular star would be rich or poor, as the case might be. Belief in astrology robbed life of any purpose and made a man a slave to an imaginary destiny. Some Talmudic passages, to be sure, show that a belief prevailed among some of the sages that human success depended upon the stars under which one was born. But we should not surrender the heritage of our own intellect. We should not believe in astrology because some person, even though he be learned, accepted it. Either he was mistaken or expressed his view allegorically. A man should never abandon his own intellectual independence. One's eyes are in his face and not in his back. One should look ahead of him and not behind him. Maimonides himself had studied all the books that dealt with astrology and became convinced that it was not a science. No true scientist ever occupied himself with astrology or ever wrote any treatises on it.[39]

He differentiated between astrology and astronomy. Astronomy was a science through which one learned of the movements of the spheres, the appearance of the new moon, and the eclipses of the sun and moon. One must admit that Maimonides was not only in advance of his own time but ahead of philosophers even in the Elizabethan age, four hundred years later, who believed in astrology.

In his rules for the application of one's reason in the

matter of accepting a dubious belief he laid down rules that remind one of the theories of Descartes, Hume and Huxley. He said that a man should be guided by the following principles: First, he should accept only that which can be positively and accurately proven, i.e., whatever can be demonstrated by the mathematical sciences; second, he should determine reality only by the evidence of one or more of his five senses; for example, he should judge color by his eyes, or decide taste by his tongue and so on; third, in religion he should believe only what he has received traditionally from the prophets and the sages.[40]

Maimonides' views on prayer are of some historical importance. He believed that the order of the various prayers was instituted by Ezra. Before the Babylonian captivity there was no fixed order of prayers. People prayed whenever the spirit moved them and whenever they wanted some wish fulfilled. After the Jews were scattered in different countries and had forgotten the Hebrew language, they voiced their prayers in the languages they spoke. Ezra, to unify the prayers, introduced the Eighteen Benedictions to be recited in Hebrew.[41] Maimonides held that one of the functions of prayer and the reading of the Law was to induce people to occupy their minds with the Precepts and to hold communion with God while divested from worldly business. Thinking about business matters during prayers renders them void.[42] He also objected to the insertion of piyyutim in the liturgy, since by reading them a man's mind might be diverted from the prayers.[43] The synagogue was a sacred place, a house of prayer, but also a place where communal work connected with charity or education should be transacted.

Maimonides considered the Hebrew language a sacred tongue. He gave explanation as to how the Andalusians came to abandon the "square" Hebrew characters in which the Torah is written, and use a different script in their ordinary writings. It was because they regarded them as too sacred for secular usage.[44] However much he loved the Hebrew language, he preferred a scholarly treatise or a good poem in Arabic or any other language to a worthless treatise or a poem without any merit in Hebrew. The subject matter was more important than the language in which it was written. One of the reasons for his seeking to eliminate the Piyyutim from the liturgy was their lack of literary merit.[45]

As for a non-scientific subject, it did not matter in what language it was written or what was the nationality of the author. A good scientific work should be read and accepted irrespective of whether it was written by a Hebrew scholar, or by a gentile.[46] He tried to explain the scarcity of Jewish scientific books on the theory that they had been lost. He maintained that the Jews in ancient times compiled not only religious works but mathematical and scientific books as well. These unfortunately had not been preserved.[47]

Maimonides held that the law served man in a double capacity; it improved him spiritually, and helped him materially. It promoted the well being of his soul by giving him sound views and valuable precepts, communicated to him according to his grade of intelligence. It ensured him material well being by properly defining the relationships in which he is to live with his fellow men. The laws of spiritual import deal with the relations between man and God; those of material interest take up those between man and man. Moses had foreseen the dangers of an extension of some of the laws and a curtailment of others, according to time, place and circumstance. Since such changes would eventually destroy the whole system of the Law and would lead people to doubt its divine origin, he issued the precaution in the Torah, "Thou should not add thereto nor diminish from it."[48]

Maimonides never doubted that the entire Jewish Law, the Written as well as the Oral, was of divine origin. The higher court, Bet Din Hagodal, the Sanhedrin, had complete authority over Jewish law, and the Jews had to follow their interpretation of it. Every Jew who accepted the Torah, had to follow the decisions of the Sanhedrin in any religious problem, it made no difference whether the Court derived the laws from tradition or deduced them by analogy.[49] Maimonides, who was himself a jurist and who wrote his book, the Mishne Torah, as a Constitution for the Jewish people of Palestine and of the Diaspora, was aware that the Law must sometimes be amended to meet the needs of time so as to harmonize religion and life. He held that an improper or obsolete interpretation of the Law by analogy could be reversed by a future court even if it had been made by a Sanhedrin. However, no other court could reverse a decision which was according to the Talmud and had been accepted by the Sanhedrin, unless the court consisted of more members and greater scholars. But since no other court could have more than seventy-one judges—the number that constituted the Sanhedrin,—it followed that it could not reverse this tribunal on such a decision.[50]

The Bet Din Hagodal (Court) had authority not only to modify a law, but to annul it or to introduce a new one. It could do this only as a temporary measure. It could enact new laws either to make a fence "around the Torah" or temporarily suspend laws during an emergency and under circumstances necessary to preserve the Jewish law as a whole. The Court could act like a surgeon who amputates a limb or removes part of a man's body to save his life.[51] Maimonides in his approval of necessary innovations by the Bet Din, followed the sages of the Second Commonwealth. With them he held that while Jewish law was divine, and was not to be lightly abrogated, yet for the purpose of law and life and to make it possible for the Jews to keep the Jewish Law, the Bet Din might amend it or even suspend it temporarily. "Temporarily" might mean a very long period. This procedure was in accord with the true historical interpretation of the development of the Jewish Law.

The judges of the court had to be learned and upright, and free even from physical defects. They particularly had to be humane, kind and merciful. Their first duty was to persuade the litigants to arbitrate their case. They could not deprive them of the right of free speech, no matter how ridiculous their cause. In arriving at their decisions, the judges had to be guided by the truth alone, regardless of how disastrously their verdict might affect one or the other of the litigants. The judge was like a physician who first tries to cure a disease by recommending a diet only, but later must resort to mild and finally even strong drugs. Similarly, as long as the judge can settle the case by advising arbitration, he should do so. Only when he sees that arbitration is hopeless, must he act according to the Law.[52]

Maimonides interpreted the principles of law relating to the Synagogue, Family and State, etc., according to historical Judaism. He also frequently cited passages from the Torah as his authority, but chiefly appealed to reason and scientific argumentation. Where the possibility of a rational interpretation was conspicuously absent, he had to base his arguments on verses of the Bible exclusively.

On the problems of Providence and Reward and Punishment, he, in the main, followed the principles of the Pharisees. He held that a man had absolute freedom in his acts and was rewarded for his upright actions and punished for his evil deeds. Animals also, had freedom of the will but they were not subject to reward or punishment.

Stoning an ox that killed a human being was a punishment directed against its owner for letting it loose. To prove that the punishment was not directed against the ox, Maimonides showed from the Talmud that the owner had no right to make any use of the ox, even to sell his skin.[53] Some of the Gaonim expressed the opinion that animals were also rewarded and punished for their acts but they took this theory from the Mutazilites; it did not represent the Jewish point of view. The rabbis prohibited cruelty to animals to teach man to be merciful and humane in general.[54]

Every rational individual was under Divine Providence, but in the case of animals only the species was, not the creature itself. Divine Providence manifested itself to man in varying degrees. It depended upon the man himself. The greater the perfection he attained, the greater the benefits extended to him. It was beneficent to those who were perfect in their conception of God, and who always directed their minds towards Him. But God permitted even those who were perfect in their knowledge of Him to enjoy His presence only when they meditated upon Him. When their thoughts were engaged in other matters, Divine Providence departed from them. The temporary withdrawal of Providence in this instance was not in the same category as its complete absence in those who do not reflect on God at all.[55]

Maimonides' views on Prophecy show his originality and have been the subject of much controversy. He held that Prophecy was a divine gift, the requisites for which were perfection of all one's faculties as well as possession of a sound body. The mind had to be cultivated, the imagination developed, and the moral sense refined. To be a prophet, one had to possess courage and intuition and to have control over sensual thoughts; no wicked or ignorant person could become one. One had to obtain special training and education. The philosophers held that Prophecy itself was an actual faculty of man that could be achieved but Maimonides maintained that only God conferred the gift. The mere possession of abilities does not make one eligible unless God bestowed upon him the gift of Prophecy.[56]

A prophet may be temporarily deprived of the power of prophecying when he is ill or depressed, for his imagination may be impaired. During mental depression, also, some of his faculties do not properly function. One of the reasons why no prophets have appeared among the Jews since their captivity was because suffering and persecution affected the faculties requisite for Prophecy. But Prophecy will be restored when Jewish suffering ceases in the Messianic Age.[57]

Maimonides classified the prophets according to their degree of endowment. Moses was the greatest prophet. He alone performed miracles in the presence of the entire people while other prophets, such as Elijah, did this in the presence of a few. Even Joshua who stayed the sun from setting, had only part of the nation as a witness to his miracle. Moses alone received his Prophecy directly from God; all the others received their messages through angels. He alone gave the Law to all the Jews, while the prophets before him (the patriarchs) taught the conception of God only to a few, and those Prophets after him, appealed to the nation to observe the Law given by Moses.

Impostors have announced themselves as prophets and announced new laws which they claimed they received by inspiration from God. Maimonides proposed a test in order to determine whether they were really prophets, and that test was abstinence from sensual pleasure. The first requisite of a prophet was contempt for sexual indulgence. Undoubtedly, Maimonides when he proposed this test had in mind the much married Mohammed.[58]

Maimonides modified his views on Resurrection, belief in which he included among the thirteen principles of Judaism in his Commentary on the Mishna. At first, he undoubtedly believed in the resurrection of the soul only and not of the body, and even then in the resurrection of the souls of the righteous only.[59] He followed the Pharisees who believed that the soul was imprisoned in the body and obtained its liberty only after death. The soul departed after the death of the body, to its own pure abode.[60] He later came to accept the view that the body would also be resurrected but he was never able to determine whether the resurrection would take place before or during the Messianic Age or after the death of the Messiah. He had to conclude that the time was unknown.[61] He had no authoritative sources for the theory of Resurrection as he had in the case of his other views. He could not prove his views from the Talmud where Resurrection is only defended by implication from the Torah.[62] Nor could he prove its truth by logic or science, nor did he find evidence in history that a dead body was ever revived, i.e. resurrected. The passage in the book of Ezekiel describing the revival of the dead in the Valley of the Bones, was allegorical.[63]

The miracle attributed to Elijah, in reviving a dead child, is deduced from the fact that the word *Va-Yamot* is a homonym, which may mean "and he is very ill," as well as "and he died". Thus the child of Zarephath had not been dead but severely ill, and Elijah cured him of his illness.[64]

Maimonides, nevertheless, accepts belief in bodily Resurrection as one of the principles of Judaism, although Resurrection was against nature and could not be proven by science. He therefore looks upon Resurrection as a miracle that may be compared to such miracles as Moses' striking the rock and causing water to gush forth.[65]

Maimonides believed in the immortality of the soul but he held that there were two species of soul, the potential intellect and the acquired intellect. The potential intellect is the soul which is given to man when he is born, and which is merely a function of the body and dies with it. The acquired intellect is the soul which is immortal. It is not a function of the body and is really separate from the body. Therefore, it does not cease to exist when the body dies. It persists forever like the other separate intelligences such as the angels and the spheres.[66]

The *Olam Haba* (The World to Come) does not mean another world which comes after this world has perished. The *Olam Haba* (The World to Come) exists in the present. It is called the *Olam Haba* because it represents the first stage of a more ideal life that follows the material life of this world.[67]

In his conception of the Messiah, Maimonides followed the general point of view held by the Jews during the Second Commonwealth. They regarded the Messiah as the deliverer of the Jews from the yoke of the gentiles. They did not believe him to be a supernatural person but a human being, a leader like King David or like Judah, the Maccabee. Only the Apocalyptical writers taught that the Messiah would have supernatural powers. The belief that the Messiah would be vested with supernatural qualities came in vogue among the Jews after the destruction of the Temple, because of the influence of Christianity. When the Jews were enduring great suffering during the Dispersion and were helpless against their oppressors, they pictured their redeemer as conquering their enemies with a "word" only. They believed that he would perform miracles.[68] Maimonides had the boldness to restore the conception of Messiah as it was current during the Second Commonwealth. He said that the Messiah would be a man, born and undergoing death like any other mortal. He would be of the family of David; he would be as wise as Solomon, and a prophet next only to Moses. He would conquer Palestine and unite the Jews there into one nation. He would rebuild the Temple and bring about the establishment of the Jewish Law. He would effect no impossible physical changes in the world. He would not perform any miracles; he would not resurrect the dead; he would be a man like the first Messiah, King David.[69]

Rabbi Akiba as well as some other sages had accepted Bar Kokba, a normal human being and a military leader, as the King Messiah. The people became convinced that Bar Kokba was not the Messiah only when he was killed. Maimonides attributed his defeat and his death to the sins of the Jewish people.

In Chapter Eleven of his Mishne Torah, Hilkot Melochim, Maimonides said that a man (king) of the family of David, who enforced the observance of the Torah among the Jews and fought the battles of God, was eligible to become the Messiah. If he succeeded in rebuilding the Temple, he assuredly was the Messiah. But, if he was neither victorious in battle nor successful in building the Temple or if he was killed, he was not the Messiah. Such a person had been sent by God only to test the people. One who was executed by the court (as was Jesus) was, therefore, not the Messiah. All the prophets had said that Messiah would redeem the Jews, gather them together and make them observe the precepts of the Torah. The followers of Jesus persecuted the Jews in his name and had them scattered over the earth. Mohammed, who came after Jesus, helped to prepare the way for the King Messiah. Maimonides was of the opinion that both Jesus and Mohammed made ready the way for the coming of the true King Messiah.

Maimonides mentions the coming of the prophet Elijah, who filled such a great role in the Talmud and in Jewish literature, only once in connection with the Messiah, and this, in reference to the part that some sages believed that Elijah would play before the arrival of the Messiah himself. He, himself, refused to emphasize the coming of Elijah because it entailed a belief in

Resurrection which was of the nature of a miracle, and because we did not know whether such a miracle might be performed after instead of before the coming of Messiah. He maintained that Prophecy would return to the Jews before the arrival of the Messiah. In his letter to the Yemenites, he fixed the year in which Prophecy would be restored to the Jews as 1216. He regarded the coming of the Messiah only as a means to a final goal just as he regarded Resurrection only as a means of reaching the *Olam Haba,* the Future World. The final goal that he looked for was the establishment of the Jewish people as a nation in Palestine, free from persecution, and able to develop their culture—the Torah. We may say that he anticipated the entire national and cultural movement which has found voice in modern Jewish History in Herzl and Ahad-Haam.

He was also very anxious to restore the institution of Semicha (ordination). He said, if all the scholars would unanimously appoint one man as a leader, he would have all the rights and privileges which the scholars possessed at the time of the Sanhedrin. That was possible only in Palestine. He believed that the restoration of the institution of Semicha would take place in Palestine before the coming of the Messiah.[70] The first Sanhedrin would be reconstituted in Galilee in the city of Tiberias.[71]

Maimonides, who lived at a time when Christian lands were regarded as the homes of Christians only and Islamic lands of Moslems only, advocated in his Constitution for the future Jewish state, equal rights for gentiles in Palestine. He maintained that under no circumstance should Jews forcibly compel them to accept the Jewish religion. The only requirement for citizenship for the gentiles was observance of the seven precepts of Noah. These seven precepts are injunctions against idolatry, blasphemy, homicide, incest, robbery, dismembering live animals, and anarchy.[72] These are not particularly Jewish laws but come under the class of *jus gentium*, the laws of society, and should be observed by every civilized person.

XII

CORRESPONDENCE WITH FRANCE

IN THE last decade of the Twelfth century, Maimonides' fame was wide-spread in Egypt. He had become the recognized authority in rabbinics; even his previous opponents accepted his decisions. He had also established himself as a successful physician.

Alkifti tells us Maimonides received a pension from the Vizier.[1] He also says that the King of the Franks in Ascalon (Richard) wanted to have him as his personal physician.[2] Maimonides, however, declined the honor. He was not anxious to live in the Christian countries where the Jews were so greatly persecuted. He preferred his adopted land. By education and by culture, he felt himself more akin to the Moslems than to the Christians.

Since he was very busy and occupied with numerous duties, he issued all the orders to be followed during the week at his home in Fostat where the Congregation used to assemble every Sabbath.[3]

It is noticeable that Judah the Exilarch who owed his post in Egypt to Maimonides was no longer mentioned in any of the later documents. He had returned to Damascus, his former residence, when Saladin again made it his capital.

Maimonides took a keen interest in Jewish affairs in Egypt. He was very active in obtaining ransom money for the many Jewish prisoners who were captured during the wars between the Moslems and the Crusaders. He wrote letters to different communities to obtain the necessary funds to release the victims.[4] With the assistance of the other rabbis, he prepared different Takkanot (ordinances) to improve the social life of the Jews in Egypt. He made a ruling that no Jew could marry in Egypt unless he produced proof that he was not already married. He also made a provision that no foreign Jew married to a girl in Egypt be permitted to leave the country even with her consent unless he gave her, to be held in escrow, a bill of divorce. Even then, he was not allowed to stay away for more than three years. Maimonides also ordained that only those who had been appointed rabbis by the court could officiate at the marriage or divorce of a couple.[5]

He, thus, sought to centralize Jewish life in Egypt. He also introduced an ordinance relating to the reading of the *Shemoneh Esreh* (Eighteen Benedictions). It had been the practise by the *Hazzan* (Cantor) to recite these prayers aloud after the congregation had silently recited them. The members of the congregation would pay no attention to him and engage in conversation. The disturbance was very annoying. Maimonides looked upon it no less than a *Hillul Hashem* (the profanation of the name of God). His sense of dignity as a Jew was wounded especially when the Moslems, whose services were orderly, used to criticize the Jews for talking during the prayers and even spitting. He, therefore, introduced a regulation compelling the members of the congregation to recite the *Shemoneh Esreh* silently at the time when the *Hazzan* chanted it.[6]

He was always very cautious in avoiding *Hillul Hashem.* He refused to reinstate a community *Shohet* (a religious slaughterer) whom he had dismissed for stealing meat in the Bazaar on the ground that he had caused *Hillul Hashem.* The gentiles who had always believed that the religious servants employed by the Jews were honest would no longer entertain this belief, if he were allowed to continue further in office. Maimonides, however, offered no objections to his practising his profession.[7]

Maimonides was very zealous in enforcing laws relating to family life. When, once, contrary to the Biblical law, a Kohen married a divorcee, Maimonides tried to persuade him to divorce her. He pronounced a ban upon them, prohibiting anyone from associating with either of them until they repented and were divorced.[8] He was particularly severe against such unions, since the offspring would be a "*Halal*" (unfit for priesthood).

However, in some decisions, Maimonides took cognizance of the circumstances of the case. In one instance, he permitted a marriage not sanctioned by the Law rather than encourage a couple to live in open immorality. An Egyptian Jew was discovered to be living with a slave girl whom he took into his home where his step-mother and her family also lived. According to the law, the man was supposed to send her away, but he could not be forced to do so. He thus could still continue his immoral relations with her. Maimonides ruled that it was better to have him free her and marry her and live with her legally rather than illegally; notwithstanding that such a marriage was against the Jewish Law, which holds that a person accused of having relations with a slave girl, cannot free her to marry her.[9]

Before the century closed, Maimonides' fame spread throughout Europe. Although his Mishne Torah, now completed, had not yet reached France, he was well known there. Some European scholars who had migrated from France to Egypt and had become Dayyanim in Alexandria, wrote letters to their former countrymen speaking highly of Maimonides. Among them were Pinhas and Meir who was a pupil of Maimonides' opponent Rabad of Posquieres, and of Abraham ben Ezra. From them, apparently, the Jews of Provence heard about his Epistle to the Yemenites (although they erroneously called this the Letter to Fez). They also now decided to appeal to him to decide on problems that perplexed them. In their case, the problems were of an intellectual nature relating to astrology which was then considered a science in Europe. They had heard the usual theories that the activities of men and the duration of their lives were foreordained by the constellations at their birth. They were baffled by conflicting passages in the Talmud on the subject. They read in some passages that life, children and livelihood depend on Mazol, stars, and not on merits. On the other hand, they found in other passages of the Talmud, statements that merit alone was a factor in life while the stars had no power over human destiny.

In 1193, they wrote in great humility to Maimonides asking him to be kind enough to solve their doubts, which they were certain he could satisfactorily do. They requested him to send his reply by a reliable person to Montpellier, situated not far from the cities of Narbonne and Marseilles, and to address it to Rabbi Jonathan Ha-Kohen who was one of the rabbis of Provençal.[10] Maimonides delayed his answer for some time, as he was very much occupied. About this time also, Saladin died and dissension temporarily arose in his family.

The Jews of Montpellier on not receiving a reply from Maimonides apparently appealed to their countryman, Pinhas, the Dayyan of Alexandria to persuade Maimonides to answer them. Pinhas did so and on the day after the Day of Atonement, the eleventh of Tishri, in the year 1195, he wrote his answer.[11]

In his letter to the Jews of Provence, he told them that apparently they had not yet received his Mishne Torah, in which he plainly stated that he regarded astrology in the light of idolatry. He hoped that his complete book which was already being studied in the East and in the West, in Yemen as well as Sicily, would eventually reach them. Meanwhile, he would give them a summary of his views. The first branch of secular learning that he had ever taken up himself was astrology and he had carefully read every book available in the Arabic language, whether original or translated. He had reached the conclusion that it was baseless and absurd, that a belief in it was tantamount to a belief in idolatry. He strongly condemned such a theory that one could read the fate of a man or his character from the stars. If this were true, that everything was foreordained, then the observance of the precepts of the Torah was unnecessary. While some passages in the Talmud implied that certain stars at the time of the birth of a person exerted an influence upon him, one should not surrender one's reason and accept a belief the falsity of which can be demonstrated by proofs. It is not known under what circumstances statements in defense of astrology were made in the Talmud and whether they were meant to be taken literally. "We should have our eyes in front of us, and not in the back." "I have revealed to you my whole heart," he added. Incidentally he corrected their error about the false Messiah in Fez and told them that he had appeared in Yemen, not in Fez, about twenty-two years earlier, that is, about 1173.[12]

While the Jews of Provence were waiting for his answer, his complete Mishne Torah had reached them, and they earnestly took up the study of this great work. The severe criticism of *Rabad*, one of their greatest rabbinical scholars, did not discourage them from making a thorough study of it. They realized that it was the product of one of the greatest scholars in Israel, and had to admit that it was even beyond their expectations. However, they did not blindly accept everything in it. Jonathan of Lunel, speaking in their behalf, sent Maimonides a letter asking him to answer twenty-four ques-

delight, strange women whom I at first took into my house as her handmaids have become her rivals and absorb a portion of my time."

Samuel ibn Tibbon, whose father Judah, inscribed his name in the history of Jewish literature as the translator of the books of Saadia Gaon, Judah ha-Levi and ibn Janah, was engaged by Jonathan and a group of admirers of Maimonides to translate the *Moreh Nebuchim* into Hebrew. Jonathan, upon receiving the first two parts of the *Moreh Nebuchim*, was favorably impressed with it and wrote a letter to Maimonides in which he thanked him and praised his work effusively. He sent this letter before he received the reply from Maimonides to the twenty-four questions, which he and his group had sent. He told him that he and his countrymen had engaged Samuel ibn Tibbon to translate the *Moreh Nebuchim* into Hebrew, and pleaded with him, in the name of the scholars of Lunel, to send the last part of the book (this part had in the meantime been sent by Maimonides). He told him that if he did not do so, they would have been wasting their money in translating an incomplete book. We thus see that they paid ibn Tibbon for his translation.[17]

When Samuel ibn Tibbon was engaged to translate the work, he did not altogether feel confident in his ability to do so, and he wrote Maimonides asking for advice and instruction. Maimonides replied that he could not at the time do this since he had just recovered from a very severe malady and was convalescing. This was apparently during the summer of 1199.[18]

When Samuel ibn Tibbon obtained the last part of the *Moreh Nebuchim*, he found himself in difficulty, for the copy had many errors. He sent a second letter to Maimonides in which after expressing his joy in his recovery, he mentioned some of the errors he found. He forwarded him part of the translation which he had made and asked him to look it over and see if it was correct, and if so to certify under his own name to that effect. He also expressed a desire to become a pupil of his, which meant, of course, that he would have to come to Egypt.[18]

Meantime, the Jews of Lunel who had learned that Samuel ibn Tibbon found difficulties in making his translation, forwarded a letter to Maimonides asking him if it was possible for him to make the translation himself.[18a]

In his answer to ibn Tibbon, Maimonides wrote that he heard a great deal about his father from European scholars who had settled in Egypt, from Rabbi Meir, the disciple of Rabbi Abraham son of David the great rabbi of Posquieres (Rabad), and that he was very much pleased to know that Judah left so worthy a son. He quoted the verses of an ancient poet, "Had they known his parentage, they would say the father's excellence has passed over to his son." He proceeded to praise the younger ibn Tibbon's Hebrew style and complimented him upon his knowledge of Arabic. He expressed surprise in discovering a man who, though born among the "stammerers," knew the Arabic language so perfectly. He also informed him that he had already received a letter from the community of Lunel that they had engaged him to make the translation. He then laid down some general rules on the art of translation.

He said that it was not only necessary for one who translates from one language to another to be familiar with both languages but also to be deeply grounded in the subject itself. "The translator should first try to grasp the sense of the subject thoroughly," he said, and then state the theme with perfect clearness in the other language. This, however, can not be done without changing the order of words, putting many words for one word, or vice-versa, and adding or taking away words, so that the subject be perfectly intelligible in the language into which he translated. This method was followed with the works of Galen, by Honein ben Is'hak, and by his son, Is'hak with the works of Aristotle. It is for this reason that all the versions of these translators are so lucid and, therefore, we ought to study them to the exclusion of all others. He added that whoever translated from one language to another literally and adhered to the order of the words and sentences found great difficulty in making a correct translation.

He then advised him as to what books on philosophy he should read. He told him to study the works of Aristotle with the help of the commentators, Alexander (Aphrodicius), Themistius or ibn Roschd (Averroes). He also suggested that he read the works on logic by Abunazr Alfarabi, especially his book, *The Principle of all Existing Things*. He dissuaded him from reading any of the philosophical works of Isaac Israeli, as all of them including his *Book of Definitions* and his *Book on the Elements* were worthless, for their author was a physician and not a philosopher.

He praised Aristotle highly. "He (Aristotle), had indeed," he wrote, "reached the highest summit of knowledge to which man can ascend unless the emanation of the Divine Spirit be vouchsafed to him, so that he attains the stage of Prophecy, above which there is no higher stage." He also advised ibn Tibbon to study the works of ibn Sina (Avicenna) although he did not think that they could be compared to the writings of Abunazr Alfarabi. He told him that he was very much pleased with the translations and that he believed that it would be of great credit to the community of Lunel. He was also glad that he had pointed out some errors. He did not encourage him to come to Egypt saying that travelling by sea incurred risk or danger and involved many difficulties. If Ibn Tibbon did come he (Maimonides) could find little opportunity to see him since he was a very busy man engaged in the affairs of the community and much occupied in the court as a physician. This letter was written in the autumn (eighth of Tishri) of 1199.[19]

At the end of 1199, or at the beginning of 1200, Maimonides finally answered the Jews of Lunel telling them that he received their first letter which they sent in the name of Jonathan, as well as the following one. In his letter to Jonathan, he said he explained why he delayed his answer to the first letter. He now told them that he had also answered all the questions which they asked in relation to his book, the Mishne Torah. He was flattered by their request that he translate the *Moreh Nebuchim* into Hebrew himself; he wished he could do so, for it would be his greatest pleasure to translate it into Hebrew. But he was no longer young and he had no time at all, being busy day and night; in fact, he scarcely found time to write the letter he was sending them and he wrote it only out of respect to their community. He advised them to have confidence in Samuel ibn Tibbon's ability to translate the book; he had just sent him a letter in Hebrew and Arabic offering suggestions in making the translation. He concluded by paying a great compliment to the Jews of France, saying that the sole hope of the Jews depended upon them, since there were very few other Jews in the entire Diaspora who occupied themselves to such an extent as they did with the study of the Talmud.[20]

Maimonides corresponded with other European scholars who had settled in Egypt, with Anatoli of Lunel,[21] and Hasdai ha-Levi, a Spaniard. In his reply to Hasdai's letter, he again set forth his views on Creation, Prophecy, Resurrection and the Precepts. Although Hasdai's letter has been lost, it is clear that it pointed out some seeming contradictions in the *Moreh Nebuchim* on these topics, particularly on the reasons for the promulgation of the precepts. Maimonides reiterated that it was certain that there was a meaning to every precept and a reason for it. The fact that the sages had inquired why the reasons for the Torah had not been revealed showed conclusively that there were reasons for the precepts, but that they were not disclosed. The remark that King Solomon understood all the reasons for the Torah except that for the sacrifice of the Red Heifer again showed that there were reasons. If the precepts had been only decrees without meaning or reason Moses would never have said, "For this is your wisdom and your understanding in the sight of the nations which shall hear all these statutes saying, surely this great nation is a wise and understanding people." For the nations would not believe that these precepts were instituted with great wisdom unless they had been promulgated with some wise purpose behind them.

Maimonides, apparently in answer to a question of Hasdai about the gentiles and the sages, had declared that the gentiles who were pious would have a share in the *Olam Haba*, providing they had attained as great a knowledge of the Creator, as was possible for a human being. He agreed with them, holding that there was no doubt that the person (gentile) who was scholarly and virtuous, and believed in a Creator, would certainly share in the *Olam Haba*. The sages in the Talmud had even said that a gentile who studied the Law of Moses was like a High Priest.[22] The fact that Maimonides wrote in a private letter that a non-Jew who admitted the Unity of God and was a virtuous and scholarly person would receive a share in the *Olam Haba*, proves indisputably his liberal and tolerant attitude towards gentiles. In this, he showed that he was in advance of his age. Christians and Mohammedans in those days did not admit that infidels had a share in their *Olam Haba* (Paradise).

At the time Maimonides wrote this letter, his son Abraham was so dangerously ill that for three days the physicians gave up hope for his recovery. He was so busy that he scarcely found time to read his correspondence. But Hasdai was apparently a very important man, for, Maimonides told him that if it were not for his admiration and love for him, he would not answer his letter. He was able to reply only because a friend agreed to copy his rough draft and forward it.

Towards the end of his life, Maimonides was very much concerned because of the havoc wrought upon the Jewish community by the falling of the river Nile to a very low level. It is apparent from his response that, as one of the leaders of the Jews of Egypt, he took their suffering very much to heart.

XIII

THE PHYSICIAN

MAIMONIDES was not only a great philosopher and a learned Talmudist, but also a well known physician whose fame had spread over the entire country. Members of the nobility as well as the common people sought his medical advice. As previously mentioned, Alkafti is authority for the statement that the King of the Franks invited Maimonides to become his physician. Abd al Latif, the well known physician of Bagdad, said that one of his reasons for spending some time in Egypt was to make the acquaintance of Musa ibn Maimun.[1] The Arabic poet and Kadhi, al Said ibn Sena al Mulk, wrote a poem in honor of Maimonides, in which he said:

Galen's art heals only the body,
But Abu-Amrun's, the body and the soul.
His knowledge made him the physician of the century.
He could heal with his wisdom, the sickness of ignorance.
If the moon would submit to his art
He would deliver her of her spots,
At the time of the full moon, cure her of her defects
And at the time of her conjunction, save her from
waning.

Maimonides practised medicine very conscientiously. He was so busy that he could not read many medical works that he wanted to. He regretted this, for as he told ibn Aknin, a lover of truth could not have sound theories on medicine unless he could prove them by reference to the proper sources. He never prescribed drugs as long as he could cure the patient by a proper diet. He resorted to drugs for his patients only when absolutely necessary.[2] He never wrote a prescription unless its efficacy was warranted by the great masters in medicine.

In his writings on medicine as in his writings on the Talmud, he used lucid language and arranged his ideas logically and systematically. He attempted to consider critically all that had been previously written on the subject. He was a voluminous writer of medical works, which were composed in Arabic, in the simple semi-philosophical style of Averroes and Avi-cenna. Some of his books were translated into Hebrew and Latin. His "Aphorisms," (*Fusul Musu*) *Pirke Moshe*, which consists of fifteen hundred Aphorisms, and is divided into twenty-four chapters, is one of his important contributions and deals with various phases of medicine. He treats here of anatomy, physiology and pathology, of aetiology, and specific therapeutics. He deals with the different causes of fever; he writes about gynaecology, the practice of personal hygiene, gymnastics, and physical training. He also discusses dietetics and drugs. In the twenty-fifth chapter, he offers a criticism of Galen. He divided this book into small chapters to make it easy to commit them to memory. He followed Hippocrates in this respect, and held that medicine was not only to be generally studied but to be memorized in detail. He wrote the Aphorisms of his book as memoranda for himself and for everyone who was to some extent familiar with medicine. He did not compile the book for specialists. He mentions four physicians, al Razi (Thazes 841-926, al Tamimi, Ali ibn Ridwan and ibn Zuhr (Aven Zoor) 1113-1199. The book was written about 1190 and translated into Hebrew in 1277.[3]

Another popular medical book that he wrote dealt with the General Rules of Health. It was dedicated to the Sultan, el Afdal, and was divided into four chapters. Maimonides paid considerable attention to rules on diet, and he stressed the importance of taking care of one's stomach. He realized the ill effects caused by constipation, and showed how it might be avoided. He issued warning against overeating to which he traced many illnesses. People do not overfeed their cattle, yet they do gorge their own stomachs. They even do not take the necessary physical exercise. Maimonides said that one should consult a physician not only when seriously ill but even when showing the slightest symptoms of illness. One should not wait until one gets dangerously sick, when it may be too late. Convalescents and elderly people, especially, should frequently consult their physicians.[4]

He did not agree with those who believed that nature alone would effect a cure and that one could altogether dispense with drugs. He said that no physician could help one whose illness was too serious for one's constitution to resist. If one's constitution could overcome the illness, one did not need a physician for nature would cure him. But when the sickness and the capacity to resist it are in the balance, then one must apply to a physician to build up one's constitution. If the physician is competent, he will be able to cure the patient by proper medical remedies, but if he is incompetent, he may break down the patient's constitution by improper treatment. Maimonides always was opposed to the administering of strong drugs. He approved of such remedies as bleeding and purgatives in emergency cases only.

He also warned against over-indulgence in coition. He expressed himself emphatically on the dangers of frequent intercourse for those who were aged and particularly those who suffered from heart ailments. He also knew the risks that convalescents took in resuming sexual relationship. He prohibited sexual intercourse immediately after meals before the food was digested, or at a time when one is hungry, thirsty, fatigued or intoxicated.

He believed that wine moderately taken was salutary to one's health. It also was a remedy in curing illness. It was more conducive to the health of older people than that of younger people. It was particular strengthening to those who were aged and feeble. Unfortunately many people indulged in it to the point of intoxication which was very injurious to the body. He demolished the false theory of those who held that intoxication once a month was beneficial to the body.[5]

In this book, he also laid great stress upon cleanliness. This was important in preserving the general health and served as an aid in healing many diseases. He also emphasized the value of breathing fresh, dry air, which was necessary to keep the body in health.

He appended fifty short paragraphs to the book as a guide to the Sultan to whom the work was dedicated. As the Sultan was a sickly and amorous man, he warned him of the dangers of overindulgence in sex, and named certain foods to be avoided which awaken sexual desire.[6]

He concluded his work saying that one should always follow the natural requirements of his own constitution in the matter of diet, physical exercise, and sexual relations. One should not change one's habits suddenly but if one had to change, one should do so gradually.

This book was written about 1198 and translated into Hebrew in 1290.

Apparently Maimonides wrote another treatise on diet for his son, in which he laid down the rules for him.

Another book of importance in seven chapters was the one on Hemorrhoids. He discussed the various foods which one afflicted with hemorrhoids should eat or avoid. He also recommended the different drugs by which to cure him. He realized that the mere cessation of the bleeding was not an indication that the disease had been cured. He warned those suffering from the malady to persist in treating it until the cure had been completed.

In this book he mentioned two physicians, Avicenna and ibn Zuhr.[7]

Maimonides also wrote a book on reptile poisons and their antidotes. This book was very important since people were often bitten by the many poisonous snakes and insects in Egypt. It was widely read in Europe and frequently referred to by physicians there. It was dedicated to the Kadhi el Fadil.[8]

He also wrote a book on Sex, in which he dealt with remedies for psychic impotence and priapism, naming certain drugs to be administered and certain foods to be eaten or avoided for a cure in either malady. He based some of his remedies upon The Canon of Avicenna.[9]

He wrote other books on medicine, one on asthma. His own activities as a physician and his daily routine are fully described in a letter to Samuel ibn Tibbon in a unique autobiographical passage:

> "I dwell at Mizr (Fostat) and the Sultan resides at Kahira (Cairo); these two places are two Sabbath days' journey (about one mile and a half) distant from each other. My duties to the Sultan are very heavy. I am obliged to visit him every day, early in the morning; and when he or any of his children, or any of the inmates of his Harem, are indisposed, I dare not quit Kahira, but must stay during the greater part of the day in the palace. It also frequently happens that one or two of the royal officers fall sick, and I must attend to their healing. Hence, as a rule, I repair to Kahira very early in the day, and even if

nothing unusual happens, I do not return to Mizr until the afternoon. Then I am almost dying with hunger. I find the ante-chambers filled with people, both Jews and Gentiles, nobles and common people, judges and bailiffs, friends and foes—a mixed multitude, who await the time of my return.

"I dismount from my animal, wash my hands, go forth to my patients, and entreat them to bear with me while I partake of some slight refreshments, the only meal I take in the twenty-four hours. Then I attend to my patients, and write prescriptions and directions for their several ailments. Patients go in and out until nightfall, and sometimes even, I solemnly assure you, until two hours and more in the night. I converse with and prescribe for them while lying down from sheer fatigue, and when night falls I am so exhausted that I can scarcely speak.

"In consequence of this, no Israelite can have any private interview with me, except on the Sabbath. On that day the whole Congregation, or, at least the majority of the members, come to me after the morning service, when I instruct (advise) them as to their proceedings during the whole week; we study together a little until noon, when they depart. Some of them return, and read with me after the afternoon service until evening prayers. In this manner I spend that day."[10]

In this letter to Aknin, he deplores the fact that his time is so taken up that he cannot pursue his studies or even read any books.

XIV

PERSONAL CHARACTER

MAIMONIDES, during the last years of his life, reached the highest position possible for a Jew in Egypt. His authority as a physician was well established and he had great influence in the court of el Fadil. He remained the same modest man that he had been in his early days in Morocco. He regarded his position as one of great responsibility and was not unduly flattered because of the personal fame and success it brought him. With his influence at Court, he did whatever he could to help his brother Jews scattered over the world. When Saladin conquered Palestine and Jerusalem, Maimonides persuaded him to permit the Jews to settle there. In his various letters, he encouraged many communities throughout the Diaspora to remain loyal to Judaism. He was very liberal with his money, being a rich man because of his jewelry business. His house was open to every Jew who came to Fostat.[1]

An aristocrat by nature, he was, nevertheless, democratic in his relations with ordinary people. In letters to friends, who had been his guests, he always remembered to send regards from his servants whom he treated as equals in his household.[2] He was devoted to his students and admirers acting towards them as a father. He always begged them to be cautious in their praise of him since they might incur the risk of personal injury or loss of their means of livelihood.[3] He showed no malice or vindictiveness towards his opponents. He had no fears that their slanderous attacks would harm him, and he forgave those who indulged in them because they profited thereby. He particularly forgave those who slandered him on account of their ignorance. He was even considerate of some of his opponents. He gave Rabbi Japhet the friendly advice not to leave Egypt where he had established himself and was safe, for some Christian country where he might be persecuted.[4]

Maimonides was a master of the art of controversy. He handled polemics with great dignity and never sought to abuse his opponents.[5] Only in his Epistle on Resurrection did he show irritation. He was angry that ignoramuses from far and wide should question his belief in Resurrection and compel him to answer them. He did not mind writing to learned men in the style he was accustomed to. He did object to lowering himself to the level of ignoramuses and writing on scholarly subject in a style as he said, suitable for women. Besides exercising great skill in polemics in the written word, he was an adept in public debate in which he frequently engaged to prove his doctrines.

Maimonides possessed great courage. When the question of faith and Judaism was involved, he disregarded all consideration for his own position or his personal safety. He fearlessly couched his views in writing even though he might be arrested for so doing by the Moslems. He wrote his letter to the Jews of Yemen at the risk of his life, since Judaism was in danger. He was ready to sacrifice himself. In his book, *Moreh Nebuchim,* he displayed outstanding boldness in openly saying that Mohammed was not the true prophet, for it must be remembered that the work appeared in a country where Islam was the dominant religion. He asked his pupil, Aknin, not to transcribe it into Arabic characters since the entire Islamic world would be able to read it and his life might be endangered. In all his writings from the Commentary on the Mishna to the *Mishne Torah,* he showed independence and heroism. He set fully forth his views although they were often antagonistic to those held by leading scholars as well as the masses. Many of his ideas were at that time considered heretical among the Jews. His ideas on the Messiah were particularly bold. He manifested great resoluteness in combating superstition and astrology. In an age when not only the ordinary people but scholars as well believed in superstition, he wielded a sharp lance against it.

His personal life was not a happy one. As a boy, he had wandered from city to city in his native country, Andalusia, in mortal fear of the fanatics (Almohades). He had been compelled to leave Spain and proceeded to Morocco where he was again in constant fear of his life from the Almohades, and had to flee from the country. When he came to Egypt, his father died and then his brother David, the main support of the family, was drowned in the Indian Ocean where all his assets were also lost. Moses had to begin life over again. Here in this country of his adoption, he was not safe since he was in constant fear of informers, for he was reputed to be a Moslem who had returned to Judaism.

Among his personal tribulations was the death of his daughter in infancy.[6] His only son, Abraham, was a sickly man.[7] He, himself, was not a strong man and frequently complained of illness. In his letter to Jonathan, he spoke of an illness that lasted more than a year. On coming home daily from his work, he used to be so exhausted that he was compelled to lie down on his couch. His body was weak and aged not because of advanced years but because of physical ailments. Although he had not yet reached three score and ten, his hands used to tremble and he found it difficult to hold a pen. He had to have physical support when he wrote his letters or when he studied.[8]

It is astonishing that one so physically indisposed who was occupied in the communal life of the Jews to such an extent and held an exalted position as physician in the Court, should have made so many contributions in various branches of scholarship, in rabbinics, philosophy, medicine and even astronomy. It is no wonder that Jews of later periods considered him almost supernatural.

Moses ben Maimon died on the twentieth of the month Tabet (the thirteenth of December) in the year 1204.[9] Both his admirers and opponents bewailed his passing and voiced their great grief. Public mourning was declared in the entire country of Egypt and for three days, Jews and Moslems, lamented. A general fast was proclaimed in Jerusalem. A portion of the Torah which is called the *Techacha* (where are given the penalties resulting from disobedience of the divine law, Leviticus, chapter twenty-six) was read in the synagogues. The *Haftora* from the first book of Samuel, concluding with the now significant verse, "The glory is departed from Israel for the Ark of God is taken," and dealing with the capture of the Ark of the Covenant by the Philistines, was also read. He was buried in Palestine in the city of Tiberas.[10]

Acording to a legend when the Jews were taking Maimonides to his burial place, Bedouins fell upon them and tried to throw the coffin into the sea, but not being able to lift it, because of its weight, although they were over thirty in number, they gave up their evil design. They decided that the coffin must contain the body of a holy man, and they not only permitted the Jews to continue their voyage to the burial place but they joined them in carrying him to his final abode.

There is current among the Jewish people the saying that from Moses till Moses (Maimonides) there arose none like Moses. We may say that this verdict of the people is the verdict of history. Moses, the son of Amram who delivered the Jews from slavery and led them to the Promised Land was the first to write a Constitution—the Torah. The second Moses (Maimonides) who likewise cherished the idea that, as a result of the wars between the Crescent and the Cross, the Jews would return to their country, Palestine, also wrote a Constitution, the second next to the Torah. The first Moses died, apparently a disappointed man because he did not enter into the Promised Land with the Jews. Moses, the son of Maimon, likewise died a disappointed man. For he did not live to see the restoration of the Jews to Palestine nor the return of Prophecy to Israel.

XV

MAIMUNISTS AND ANTI-MAIMUNISTS

THE great admiration felt for the *Mishne Torah* and the *Moreh Nebuchim* by the Jewish community of Lunel and other towns in Provence, was not unanimously shared. It will be recalled that Abraham ben David RaBaD, one of the outstanding scholars in Provence, criticised the *Mishne Torah* very severely, particularly the interpretations of the Halachot.

Meir, the son of Todros Abulafia, of Toledo, Spain, was greatly opposed to some of the ideas of Maimonides, particularly those on Resurrection and the Incorporeality of God, and about 1200, not long before Maimonides died, he sent a letter to the community of Lunel directed against the *Mishne Torah.* He, indeed, showed great courage in openly attacking it. Although only a young man, still in his twenties,[1] he defied the general sentiment which was then sympathetic towards Maimonides' views.

Liberalism and heresy prevailed at the time in Provence among both Jews and Christians. Aristotelian philosophy was then studied in Provence. The heretical sect of the Albigensians was dominant, and exerted a great influence upon the Jews. The Jewish communities were under the control of liberal men like Jonathan of Lunel and others. The fundamentalists, who believed literally in the Bible, could not counteract their liberal influence. The letter of Meir Abulafia, hence, really had no effect upon the Jews of Provence. He was even rebuked in a letter by Rabbi Aaron, the son of Meshullam, who told him that his letter was childish and that he had besmirched the name of one of the greatest leaders in Israel. To charge Maimonides with not believing in Resurrection and other matters, showed a lack of understanding of his works. As a matter of fact, said Rabbi Aaron, there was no one in Israel since the Talmud had been concluded, who was Maimonides' equal.[2]

Sheshet, the son of Isaac of Barcelona, wrote a letter to the community of Lunel full of indignation at Meir Abulafia for daring to criticize Maimonides. He called Meir an ignorant man; he was an obscurantist and, thus, belied his name, Meir, the enlightener. Sheshet defended Maimonides' belief that the soul only and not the body would be resurrected. He explained that the reason why the Talmud in many passages sponsored a belief in bodily Resurrection, was because it was an inducement to the common people who could not comprehend disembodied existence, to accept Judaism in its entirety. Similarly, as some Arabic scholars had informed Sheshet, the Moslem conception of a Future Paradise full of beautiful houris was an incentive to the ordinary people to accept the Moslem religion and the Prophet. The *Mishne Torah* was a work of extreme importance and the reason that some of the Judges in

Castile objected to it was that their status as sole arbiters of the Jewish Law was undermined since its appearance. As the book was written in very simple language, the people would be able to read the decisions given and thus be independent of the Judge.[3] Though Sheshet was a student of philosophy and science, and well versed in Arabic literature, he was not the equal of the man he attacked, in knowledge of Rabbinical lore.[4]

Rabbi Samson of the city of Sens, was likewise critical of Maimonides' work. He, apparently, showed his displeasure at Maimonides' heretical views in refusing to meet the philosopher's son, Abraham, by changing his course when visiting Palestine in 1211, and taking the route to Acco so as to avoid Egypt, where Abraham lived. The other rabbis in whose company he left France went by way of Egypt. Whatever was the real motive for this unwarranted change of itinerary, the son of Maimonides felt hurt that Samson avoided Egypt on his way to Palestine. We do know that Samson, during his stay in Palestine, criticized the works of Maimonides.[5]

In the Orient at that time, another critic of Maimonides, Daniel of Damascus, one of the pupils of Samuel ben Ali of the Yeshivah of Bagdad, continued his teacher's attacks upon the Rambam. Joseph Aknin was sharply incited against him for this, and wrote a letter to Abraham, son of Maimonides, then the Nagid of Egypt, to use his authority to have Daniel excommunicated. Abraham did not do so because he could not act without bias, being the son of the man whom Daniel had attacked, and because Daniel was after all, a religious man who differed with Maimonides, his father, in only a few details, notably, on the question of demons. But, Daniel was finally excommunicated for his attacks upon Maimonides by David, the Exilarch of Damascus. He later regretted his assaults.[6]

These controversies over Maimonides served only as a prelude to those which took place before and after the third decade of the Thirteenth century. The Jews became divided into two hostile camps, who fought each other, not only with excommunications and counter-excommunications but even engaged in physical combats.

Solomon, the son of Abraham, and Rabbi of the city of Montpellier, was the representative of the fundamentalist group. With the help of his two students, David, the son of Saul, and Jonah of Gerona, he issued excommunications against those who studied the *Moreh Nebuchim* and the *Sefer ha-Mada* (the first book of the *Mishne Torah*) or engaged in any other secular studies. These excommunications brought about counter-excommunications from the adherents of Maimonides.

The Jewish population, at the time, was divided into several groups of which two opposing factions commanded the most attention. The radicals who were much influenced by the teachings of Aristotle, as well as by the ideas of the heretical Albigensians, sought to change the Jewish religion. They maintained that the entire Torah was allegorical, and even denied the historical existence of Abraham and Sarah. They believed that Abraham represented matter while Sarah represented form, and held too, that the Twelve Tribes were in re-

slandering Maimonides. Bahye forwarded his letter of excommunication to other communities, directing them to issue similar bans against these three men. The communities of Monzon, Huesca, Calatayud and Lerida, did so. Bahye also sent a personal letter to the same effect to the communities of Aragon. For these men had dared attack the *Mishne Torah*—"the strong hand (Yad ha-Hazaka) the great Vision which Moses performed before the eyes of the entire Jewish people."[10] These men, moreover, had been responsible for the excommunication issued by the Rabbis of France against all those who read the *Moreh Nebuchim*, the *Sefer ha-Mada* and secular books.

As a result of these excommunications and counter-excommunications, the Jewish communities of Provence, as well as of Spain, were in constant turmoil. A young man in Spain who had already established a reputation as one of the greatest Talmudic scholars, Moses, the son of Nahman (Nahmanides)—Ramban (born 1194, died about 1270) sought to bring these controversies to a conclusion. His role was largely that of arbitrator and conciliator. He entered on the scene upon receiving a letter from Meir Abulafia, invoking his aid in behalf of Solomon, now so sorely harassed. Meir Abulafia, who thirty years previously had written a letter to the community of Lunel protesting against the writings of Maimonides, in letter to Ramban (Moses ben Nahman) heralded Solomon as a hero for his courage in attacking heretics in general, and absolved him from attacking in particular, Maimonides personally. For thirty years, and from Louis the Ninth, the Saint, to the heresies entertained by the radical Jews in France. If they would only turn to God, He would perhaps release the French Jews from their sufferings. Judah especially attacked Samuel ibn Tibbon because of his translation of the *Moreh Nebuchim* into Hebrew and held him also responsible for the prevailing heresy. He concluded by saying that his own anger was directed against the scum of the Maimunists although he was aware that there were scholars among them who, unfortunately, had no influence upon the rabble.[16]

Though Judah was opposed to the *Moreh Nebuchim*, he never uttered a word against the *Sefer ha-Mada*, the first book of the *Mishne Torah*, although it contained many of the theological ideas found in the *Moreh Nebuchim*. He regarded the *Mishne Torah* in its entirety, as a masterpiece.

In a letter to one of the Rabbis of Spain, Solomon, in behalf of himself and his students, presented their side of the controversy. As a matter of fact, they had entered it only out of zeal for God, to combat those in Montpellier who sought to destroy tradition and said that most of the Bible was allegorical and that the Precepts were no longer binding. These heretics spread the rumor that he had attacked Maimonides, hoping thus to arouse all the admirers of the great thinker against him. But, he never had spoken against him. He merely appealed to the Rabbis of France to rally to his aid when he saw that he could not combat his enemies single-handed. This they did by putting a ban against the reading of the *Moreh Nebuchim*. The Maimunists then sent embassies to the various communities to incite the masses against him and his two students. They sent David Kimhi to Spain to stir up trouble just as they themselves had previously done in Provence. Solomon appealed to the Spanish Jews not to give credence to the fabricated statements that he had put a ban upon anyone who followed Maimonides.[17]

Moses ben Nahman, Nahmanides (Ramban) again entered upon the scene with a second letter and sought to reconcile the two hostile groups. He first cleared Maimonides from any suspicion of heresy, for his strict observance of the Law had never been doubted. He had done more for Judaism in his country than any other Rabbi. By his influence in Court, he had destroyed the power of the Karaites. Through his books, he made it possible to study philosophy from Jewish sources without going to Aristotle. He spoke very highly of the *Mishne Torah* not excepting the *Sefer ha-Mada* to which some people objected because it stated that God was not corporeal. No exceptions to this book were valid for such a reason, for other Jewish thinkers, Saadia Gaon among them, had taken a similar position.

Nahmanides was, however, critical of the *Moreh Nebuchim* which he said should not be publicly studied. In fact, Maimonides himself said that the book was not for the masses. Nahmanides then advised the Rabbis of France to remove their ban against the study of philosophy and adopt some more rational measures for the extirpation of heresy. They could not make the entire

Jewish people pious by a decree. Those who had devoted themselves to their studies would not desist from them in spite of all the bans. The Rabbis might demand that they give up philosophy, but could not force them to do so.[18]

The feud between the two groups in Montpellier reached such a point that Rabbi Solomon in 1233 approached the Papal legate, and the Dominicans and the Franciscans for aid in suppressing the *Moreh Nebuchim*. There was no doubt as to the eventual success of his plan. For the Council of the Ecclesiastical Province of Sens held in Paris in 1210, had already prohibited the reading of the works of Aristotle on pain of excommunication. And in 1215, Robert de Courçon, the Papal legate, renewed the prohibition in the following words—NON LEGANTUR LIBRI ARISTOTELIS DE METAPHYSICA ET DE NATURALI PHILOSOPHIA, NEC SUMMAE DE EISDEM.[19]

Solomon pointed out to the Dominicans and the Franciscans that the *Moreh Nebuchim* contained the entire Aristotelian theory and should, therefore, be burned. They listened with sympathy to his appeal and were moved by the force of his arguments with the result that they consigned Maimonides' works to the flame.[20] A bon-fire was now made of all copies they could collect. The news of this spread, and kindled the indignation of many Jewish communities. Those who had hitherto been neutral and even those who had supported Solomon, now abandoned him. Kimhi who had returned from his fruitless mission in Spain addressed another letter to Judah al Fakhir. He said that he bore no malice against him for having rebuked him and called him "David the little." What he wanted to know now was whether he would support such a wicked informer as Solomon. He was amazed that Judah had called such a malefactor, a pious man—had praised a scoundrel who had asked the gentiles to destroy Jewish heretics as they did their own. He begged Judah in the name of God, to excommunicate Solomon and his two disciples. "They have now no support but you," he said, "all the Rabbis of France have left them."[21]

Judah al Fakhir replied that he had never intended to humiliate Kimhi. He had used severe language against him only because he was apprehensive that a schism was breaking out in Judaism, as a result of the controversy. Though Rabbi Solomon of Montpellier was seriously at fault for what he had done, his opponents were to be blamed for the unseemly policy he had adopted. They had so embittered him that he had acted without realizing the serious consequences of his act.[22]

Some of David Kimhi's friends, among them Meshullam, the son of Kolonymos, came to his defense. Meshullam, though an admirer of al Fakhir, protested to him against the insulting tone of his first letter to a man like David Kimhi who was a scholar. Al Fakhir soon apologized and said that he would never again insult Kimhi. The news of the burning of the *Moreh Nebuchim* continued to be bruited and aroused serious protests.[23]

Joseph, the son of Todros ha-Levi of Burgos, Spain (the brother of Meir ha-Levi), sought to reconcile the two belligerent groups in Montpellier, in a letter which he sent to the community. He appealed to the Jews there not to condemn Solomon because he criticized the *Moreh Nebuchim.* He had a right to do so since it was not a sacred book which was revealed like the Torah to Moses on Mount Sinai. Solomon rightly protested against the admirers of the *Moreh Nebuchim* because they were the ones who forsook Judaism. Undoubtedly, he had made a grievous mistake in approaching the Christians and asking them to burn Maimonides' books in Montpellier. He blamed the Maimunists for arousing dissension among the Jews in Provence. They were now seeking to foment quarrels among the Jews in Spain as well, and for this purpose had sent David to Burgos. He told the Jews of Montpellier that the letters which David Kimhi brought with him had not been signed by their important Rabbis but by men of no significance who did not represent the sentiment of the community. He begged them to cease their bickerings—not to concern themselves about the recent events, for, what was done could not be undone.

At the same time, Joseph, the son of Todros, praised Maimonides very highly. He was the greatest scholar since Rab Ashi, the compiler of the Talmud. His *Mishne Torah*, including the *Sefer ha-Mada*, was one of the outstanding works in Rabbinical literature. Joseph also paid his respects to the *Moreh Nebuchim*, but said that Maimonides wrote it as a guide for students of philosophy who became perplexed and not for ordinary people who do not study and, therefore, have no intellectual problems. He compared the ignorant man who undertakes the study of the *Moreh Nebuchim*, to one who goes upon a diet unsuitable to him, that may be followed by fatal results. He particularly blamed Samuel ibn Tibbon and Judah Harizi for translating the *Moreh Nebuchim* into Hebrew. Many ignorant people, not prepared for philosophical thinking had since come to believe that they became philosophers by reading the *Moreh Nebuchim.* Maimonides himself had thought of suppressing the third part in which he dealt with the reasons for the promulgation of the Precepts, but it was too late, for the book had already been circulated in many countries. The truth of the matter was that no reasons for the promulgation of the Precepts should be revealed to the masses. The Talmud had defended this point of view.[24]

Samuel, the son of Abraham Sasportas, wrote a letter to the Rabbis of France wholly in defense of Maimonides. He protested against the burning of the books, calling it a profanation of the name of God. He tried to uphold the philosophical ideas of Maimonides on the Incorporeality of God and Resurrection, and he said that if the Rabbis of France had any criticism to make against his teachings, they should do so, but they should destroy his arguments by reason, and not ban his books. He saw no ground for one of the chief objections raised by the Rabbis against Maimonides, namely that he assigned reasons for the promulgation of the Precepts. The Talmud itself implied that there were reasons for the Precepts when it said that they had not been revealed.

In fact, Rabbi Simon, one of the Talmudic sages, had given some reasons for numerous verses (Samuel was mistaken, for Rabbi Simon does not give the reasons for the verses of the Bible, but interpreted the spirit of the laws). Samuel also wondered why the Rabbis objected so much to Maimonides' assigning an idolatrous origin to sacrifice when the Midrash itself had advanced a similar theory.[25]

Other defenders of Maimonides arose. Judah and Abraham, the sons of Hasdai, sent letters to the Jewish communities in Spain, bitterly condemning Solomon and his followers in no uncertain terms. They appealed to them to sustain the Jews of Provence in their fight on behalf of Maimonides. They complained that the community of Burgos alone supported the Maimunists of Provence.[26]

When in the winter of 1235, Abraham the son of Maimonides, heard of the burning of his father's books, he was naturally greatly grieved. He wrote a letter challenging the objections of the Anti-Maimunists against his father's views. He said that his father had never intended to lay down his theory of the origin of the Precepts as the final word. Abraham did not mention the names of his father's admirers who had written to him about the burning of the books as he felt he might endanger their lives.[27] Had he given their names, the Anti-Maimunists would have informed against them as heretics to the church authorities. Information to the authorities on heresy was given at that time by the devotees of all the religions; such an act was highly ex-

prohibiting any one, on pain of excommunication, from reading the *Moreh Nebuchim.* Public opinion was, however, against him. David, the Exilarch of Mosul, excommunicated him and issued a ban against any one who would slander Maimonides. Jessee of Damascus and Samuel Kohen, the head of the Yeshiva of Babylon, issued similar decrees.[34] Thus, they put an end to Solomon Petit's agitation against Maimonides' works. It is possible that it was at this time that some of the followers of Solomon Petit put on the tombstone of Maimonides, "Here is buried Moses, the son of Maimon, who was excommunicated and was a heretic."

The Exilarch of Damascus sent letters to the Jewish communities in Europe informing them that Solomon Petit had been excommunicated for slandering Maimonides. The Anti-Maimunists now tried to win recruits to their cause. The Maimunists took action to combat their efforts. Hillel, one of them, of the city of Verona, who had settled in Italy, wrote a letter to Isaac of Rome, physician to Pope Boniface, the Eighth, appealing to him not to support the Anti-Maimunists. He gave a complete account of the entire controversy which had started about sixty years previously in Montpellier. He spoke of the burning of the Talmud which, undoubtedly, was retribution on the Jews for the burning of the books of Maimonides. Suspecting that Isaac himself might have entertained doubts about the *Moreh Nebuchim*, he offered to clear them up to his satisfaction. He also ventured a solution to settle the entire controversy. He proposed organizing a committee in Alexandria to send out an invitation to all the communities of Germany and France for the purpose of fixing a meeting in Venice, Marseilles or Genoa to discuss the merits of the case. If the Anti-Maimunists were right, Maimonides' books should be put out of sight. If they were wrong, they should accept the decree of the Rabbis of Egypt and Babylon, never to attack or slander him again.[35]

While this controversy was taking place in Palestine, another feud started in France. Abba Mari of Montpellier attracted attention as one of the leading agitators against Maimonides' writings. Jacob, the son of Machir ibn Tibbon, and Judah, the son of Abraham of Beziers, took up cudgels in defense of the great teacher. Abba Mari appealed for support to Solomon ibn Adret, Rabbi of Barcelona, the outstanding Rabbi of the time. Solomon heeded his request and on July 31, 1305, declared a ban signed by more than thirty other Rabbis against any one who studied science, except medicine, before he reached the age of twenty-five.[36] In this ban, neither the name of Maimonides nor the title of his books was mentioned. It was directed rather against the radicals who interpreted the Scriptures allegorically. In retaliation, Rabbi Jacob of the family of ibn Tibbon, issued a counter-ban against any one who hindered students under twenty-five from studying science or against any one who slandered Maimonides. Since the books of Maimonides were not mentioned in the ban of ibn Adret, it was interpreted as not affecting them. The Maimunists, however, tried to show the people that ibn Adret included them in the general condemnation though he did

It is strange that though he was a nationalist himself Smolenskin did not detect any nationalistic idea in Maimonides, but his oversight here was in no wise different from that of all the other modern Hebrew thinkers, Ahad Haam included. Maimonides, however, was not chauvinistic in his nationalism. He admired scholarship even outside of the Jewish nation. Curiously enough, it may be for this supposed lack of nationalistic sentiment that Smolenskin felt animosity towards Maimonides.

XVI

HIS INFLUENCE

MAIMONIDES' influence has never been fully estimated. His writings have colored the trend of thought among theologians of the two great religions, Islam and Christianity. When the *Moreh Nebuchim* was transcribed into the Arabic characters soon after its completion, it took hold upon the Mohammedan world. Abdel Latif, a contemporary Moslem theologian, read it.[1] Arabic scholars lectured upon it to their pupils, and generally extolled it except the section dealing with the theories on Prophecy.

Maimonides' influence upon Christian theologians was even more significant. As a result of the capture of Constantinople by the Fourth Crusade in 1204, and the consequent revelation of the treasures of Greek literature to European scholars, the Church in the Thirteenth Century paid considerable attention to the writings of Aristotle. Through commentaries of Averroes, who owed his fame to the Jewish translation of his works, Christian theologians were introduced to Maimonides who made a profound impression upon their thought.

The Scholastics read and studied his *Moreh Nebuchim* extensively. Alexander of Hales (died 1245)

They would not believe that the author of the *Mishne Torah* wrote them.

The authority of Maimonides became so great that even the Kabbalists tried to claim him as one of themselves. They maintained that he became a Kabbalist in the last days of his life. Shem-tob ben Abraham ibn Gaon of Segovia, Spain, who wrote a commentary on the *Mishne Torah*, said that he read in an old scroll in Maimonides' own handwriting a statement of his belief in Kabbalistic ideas.[12]

Maimonides' influence penetrated many movements in Jewish history. When, in the Sixteenth century, an attempt was made to revive the act of *Semicha* (Ordination) in Palestine, its leader, Jacob Berab found authority for so doing in Maimonides' assertion in the *Mishne Torah* that *Semicha* would be reinstated before the coming of Messiah, if done so unanimously by the Palestinian scholars.[13] Some of the Orthodox Rabbis in more recent times, sought justification for joining the Zionist movement in Maimonides' statement in the *Mishne Torah* that a Jewish court would be established in Palestine before the arrival of Messiah. They also discovered in his writings proof of the establishment of a Jewish State through the natural course of historical development rather than through supernatural means.

In the field of Rabbinics, Maimonides' sway over Judaism was still greater. Solomon Adret, an Anti-Maimunist, who put a ban on secular studies, considered the *Mishne Torah* without parallel in Rabbinical literature. Later Rabbis followed Maimonides' system of compilation. The authors of the *Tur* and the *Shulhan Aruk* used the *Mishne Torah* as their model. Rabbis copied his ideas verbatim without even naming their source. They avoided mentioning his name as he did the sages of the Talmud and the Gaonim. Menahem ben Zerah copied verbatim the reasons for the promulgation of the Precepts from Maimonides, but he did not allude to him by name.[14] Menahem, the son of Solomon ha-Meire, another Rabbi of the Thirteenth century, quoted him without mentioning him.[15]

The Maimunist controversy, which began during his lifetime, has not yet ceased, as many Jews still object to some of his doctrines, particularly his reasons for the Precepts in the third part of the *Moreh Nebuchim.* A controversy so enduring could have been inaugurated only by the writings of a Talmudic scholar. Scholars and thinkers may have passing influence upon some intellectuals; they may have followers and opponents, but only for a limited time. The philosophical writings of men like Abraham ibn Ezra, and Levi ben Gershon, have been almost completely ignored by the bulk of the Jewish people; they were not Talmudic authorities like Maimonides.[16]

The *Mishne Torah* became the standard book in Jewish Law. Commentaries and even books were written about it. Rules on how to study it were laid down by Rabbinical scholars.[17] Some Rabbis in their reverent admiration, have since maintained that there are no contradictions in it. Where such seemed to exist, the Rabbis

NOTES

CHAPTER I

[1] In Arabic Literature he was known as Abu Imran Musa ben Maimun ibn 'Abd Allah. According to the *Sefer Yuhasin*, Maimonides was born on a Saturday, comp. *Shalshelet ha-Kabbala.*

[2] At the end of his commentary on the Mishna, Maimonides named seven of his ancestors who bore the title Dayyan, as follows: Moses, son of Maimon; Dayyan, son of Joseph Hacham; son of R. Isaac Dayyan; son of Joseph Dayyan; son of R. Obadiah Dayyan; son of R. Solomon the Rabbi; son of Obadiah Dayyan; Aaron ben Meshulam in his letter to Meir ha-Levi said that he had heard that Maimonides' ancestry is traced back to R. Judah ha-Nasi of the family of David.

[3] *Shalshelet ha-Kabbala.*

[4] See also *Shevet Jehuda* by Solomon ibn Verga.

[5] Comp. Geiger, *Ozar Nehmad I*, page 97. It is very likely that Joseph Kimhi was still very young when he fled from Spain. His son David, later was one of the greatest admirers of Maimonides.

[6] *Moreh Nebuchim* II, 9.

[7] See the introduction to *Zedah la-Derech.*

[8] *Maamar ha-ibur, Kobez* II, p. 17.

[9] *Makalah fi-Sinaat al-Mantik.* This brochure was written by him before he reached his twentieth birthday. It was translated by Moses ibn Tibbon. It is edited by M. Chmizer, *Festschrift Cohen*, 191.

[10] Comp. the end of Maimonides' Commentary on the Mishna.

CHAPTER II

[1] See Munk, "*Notice sur Joseph ben Iehouda,*" pp. 42-44. Graetz, (Hebrew). Vol. IV. p. 332.

[2] Friedlander, "Introduction to the Guide," p. XVIII. Also Margoliouth, *JQR*. O. S. XIII, p. 539.

[3] *Sefer Hasidim*, p. 64.

[4] Ibid.

[5] Comp. Luzzatto, *Ozar Nehmad*, p. 173-178.

[6] Saadia ibn Danun, *Hemdah Genuzah*, p. 30.

[7] Ibid. I, p. LXXIV-LXXII.

[8] *Ab. Zarah*, 18b, ibid. 16b.

[9] *Taanit,* 25b.

[10] This letter was published in *Kobez* II, p. 12. See also *Hemdah Genuzah,* I, p. 613. There are some who doubt the authenticity of this letter. However, it is very evident that Maimonides compiled it. It is quoted by *Rivash,* (Isaac hen Sheshet), II and *Tashbaz,* (Simon ben Zemah Duran), 63a.

[11] Responsum 369. Ed. A. Freimann.

[12] *Sefer Haredim* by Eleazar Askari, p. 61. This is quoted in the name of Samuel Shkeil who copied this from a manuscript of the Rambam found in Acco.

[13] Comp. his commentary on the Mishna.

[14] *Sefer Haredim,* Ibid.

[15] According to Saadiah ibn Danun, Maimun and his sons first went to Alexandria and then later to Jerusalem. From Palestine, Maimonides returned to Egypt (*Hemdah Genuzah*). S. Eppenstein (*Moses ben Maimon,* II. p. 24) follows Saadiah ibn Danun, maintaining that the account found in the *Sefer Haredim* is not authentic. He argues that the Rambam usually gives the dates according to the Era of Contracts whereas in this case the dates are according to the Era of Creation. Eppenstein, however, overlooked the fact that this document was written by Maimonides during his stay in Palestine where the Era of Contracts was never used. There, all records were kept according to the Era of the Creation. Only in the Diaspora was the System of reckoning according to the Era of Contracts used.

CHAPTER III

[1] Comp. Benjamin of Tudela, ed. Asher.

[2] See Sambari, Neubauer, *Medieval Jewish Chronicles,* Vol. I, p. 115. See Mann. *The Jews in Egypt and in Palestine under the Fatimid Caliphs,* Vol. I, p. 251-52, and the literature there quoted; also Berliner's, *Magazin,* 1890.

[3] Mann, ibid. p. 235. According to Mann, Samuel died soon after 1159.

[4] Comp. *Megillat Zuta,* edited by D. Kahana, in *Haschiloah,* Vol. XV pp. 175-184. See the same *Megillah,* ed. by Wertheimer in *Ginze Yerushalaim,* Vol. I, under the title *Megillat Mizraim.* Comp. Mann, ibid.

[5] Commentary on the Mishna, Abot. Ch. IV.

[6] Comp. *Bibl. Arabico-Hispana,* p. 293, "gemmarum, aliarumque ejusmodi rerum mercatura victum quaeritans."

CHAPTER IV

[1] Comp. the end of Maimonides' Introduction. Comp. also Graetz (Hebrew) Vol. IV, p. 339 Note 2.

[2] Frankel, *Darke ha Mishna.* Also, *Zedah la Derech,* by Menahem ben Zerah.

[3] See *Ber.* 18b.
[4] *Sanh.* 99a.
[5] *Ned.* 8b.
[6] Albo, *Ikkarim.*
[7] *The Eight Chapters,* was edited by Joseph Gorfinkle, N. Y. 1912.
[8] Aristotle Ch. IV. See Ibn Gabirol, "*Tikkun Middot ha Nefesh.*" Aristotle, ibid. I, 13. "Now if this is so, clearly it behoves the statesman to have some acquaintance with psychology, just as the physician who is to heal the eye or the other parts of the body must know their anatomy. Indeed a foundation of science is even more requisite for the statesman, inasmuch as politics is a higher and more honourable art than medicine."
[9] Comp. Mishneh Torah, *Hilkot Deot.*
[10] *Nic. Eth.* II.
[11] *Abot,* II, 12.
[12] *Nic. Eth.* VII.
[13] Comp. *Sifra,* 184, (ed. Venice).
[14] Comp. Gorfinkle, *The Eight Chapters,* and literature there quoted. For the ethics of Maimonides see Rosin's, *Ethik des Maimonides,* 1876.
[15] *Ab. Zorah* V; *Ket.* I; See also, *Mik.* IV.
[16] *Sota* II; *Kid.* I; *Zab.* II; *Mik.* IV.
[17] Comp. *Parah,* III, *Maksh.* VI.
[18] See The Introduction, also *Shebu.* VI.
[19] Yellin and Abraham's *Maimonides,* 1903, p. 71.
[20] The Introduction was translated by Judah Harizi. Most of the Commentary was translated about the year 1298. See Graetz (Hebrew) V. 249. Also Steinschneider, *Hebraeishe Uebersetzungen,* II, p. 923. The Commentary has been printed in the different editions of the Talmud. It was also translated into Latin. The Introduction and some parts of the Commentary were edited by Ed. Pocockle, 1655, *Porta Mosis.* There are some modern critical editions of the Arabic text with a Hebrew translation, Hamburger, Berlin, 1902. The Commentary to the Section *Tohorot* was edited by J. Derenbourg, 1887. The introduction to *Helek* was edited by Holzer, 1901.

CHAPTER V

[1] Gustav Weil, *Geschichte der Chalifen,* III, 328. Stanley Lane—Pool, *Saladin,* N. Y. 1898.
[2] Ibid.
[3] Ibid.
[4] Lane-Pool, ibid.
[5] Ibid.
[6] See, *Megillat Zuta Haschiloah,* 1905. p. 181. Neubauer, *JQR.* O.S. IX. Mann, "*The Jews in Egypt.*" I, 234.

CHAPTER VI

[1] Written in Arabic and translated into Hebrew by Ibn Tibbon about the year 1210, see Steinschneider, *Heb. Ueber.* p. 930. See Jacob Mann, *Hatekufah* 1928; Fritz Baer, *Monatsschrift f. G.* 1926.

[1a] Maimonides considered Jesus a Jew, because his mother was a Jewess. This is according to the reading of the manuscript of the Jewish Theological Seminary.

[2] According to *Ket.* 50a, the Jew may not give more than a fifth of his wealth to charity.

[3] Abu Isa Obadiah (744-750).

[4] Weil, *Geschichte;* Lane-Pool, *Saladin.*

[5] See the letter of Rambam, *Kobez,* III, 9.

[6] Kaufmann, *REJ.* XXIV, Comp. Bacher, Ibid. XXXIV. Israel Levi, ibid. XXXIII.

[7] Graetz, (Hebrew) IV, p. 348.

[8] The letter was published in *Kobez,* II, 137. Also by Geiger, *Moses ben Maimon.* According to Graetz, this letter to Jophet was written not later than 1170, since Maimonides used the expression "I am in a strange country." Graetz maintains that he could not have used such an expression when he was already well established. The letter, however, was written *eight years after,* about 1182, and Maimonides might have used the expression "I am in a strange country," because he never regarded Egypt as his native country and always signed himself, Moses, the Spaniard.

[9] *Bib. Arab. Hispanae,* 293.

CHAPTER VII

[1] Weil, *Geschichte;* Lane-Pool, *Saladin.*

[2] Ibid.

[3] According to Sambari, *Medieval Hebrew Chronicles,* Judah the Exilarch was a resident of Damascus. Mann (text I) notes that it is not known when Judah settled in Fostat. Now, however, this is quite evident.

[4] See, *Megillat Zuta.*

[5] *Responsa.* Ed. Freimann, 1934, p. 192.

[6] Ibid, pp. 91-96.

[7] Ibid. p. 100.

[8] *Kobez,* II, 37.

CHAPTER VIII

[1] According to Maimonides, Judah was the first to put the Mishna in writing.

[2] According to L. Ginzberg, *JE.* 1, RABaD opposed Maimonides for setting up the incorporeality of God as a dogma in Judaism.

[3] *Ishut.* Comp. Responsum, p. 161. Ed. Freimann, also, *Birchat Abraham,* ed. Goldberg, p. 61.
[4] *Maachalot Asurot,* Comp. also Targum Jonathan, Deut. XIV, 21. Also *Midrash* to Lev.
[5] *Tumat Met,* I.
[6] *Hobel W-Mazik,* VII.
[7] Ibid. See also B.K. 98a.
[8] *Naaroah Betulah,* I.
[9] *Gerushin,* XIII, Maimonides gave a lenient interpretation of the law of Aguna.
[10] *Mechirah,* V.
[11] *Gerushin,* I.
[12] *Mechirah,* I.
[13] Ibid. II, Comp. *Malweh we-Loweh;* on *Asmakta* in the Tannaitic literature. See S. Zeitlin, *JQR.* 1929.
[14] *Genebah,* V. This reading differs with the commentators on the *Mishne Torah,* but it is according to the reading of the *Tur,* which is the correct one, as can be proven by internal evidence.
[15] *Malweh we-Loweh,* comp. Baba Mezia, 82a.
[16] *Malweh we-Loweh,* III.
[16a] *Ned.* III, 10.
[17] *Edut.* XX.
[18] *Hobel u Mazik,* VIII. This law is not to be associated with the case found in Talmud B.K. 116b. Comp. RABaD, l.c.
[19] *Rozeah,* II, Cf. *Moreh Nebuchim,* III, 40.
[19a] *Genebah,* I.
[20] *Toen we-Nitan,* III; *Sechirut,* XI.
[21] *Malweh we-Loweh,* XV. He must only take an oath that he had paid.
[22] He was not well-versed in geography either, Comp. *Responsa,* ed. Freimann, p. 311.
[22a] See *Isure Bi'ah,* XIII.
[23] *Parah Adumah,* I
[23a] A. Schwarz, Das Verhaltnis Maimun's zu den Gaonen, *Moses ben Maimon,* I. pp. 332-410.
[24] *Malweh we-Loweh,* XV.
[24a] *Tumat Zaraat* XV, also *Mikwaot,* XI.
[25] *Kobez,* 1, 25.
[25a] Ibid. 12.
[26] Ibid, 11, 30.
[26a] Comp. Blau, Das Gesetzbuch des Maimonides, Historisch betrachtet, *Moses ben Maimon,* II, pp. 331-358. See Tchernowitz, *Miklat,* 1920.
[27] *Maasseh ha-Korbanat,* II.
[27a] Men. 45.
[28] See, his Commentary on the Mishna, Sanh. also *Hilkot, Melachim.*
[29] The idea of a constitution has been well defined. "L'ensemble des

institution et des lois fondamentales, destinees a regler l'action de tous les citoyens". Holland, *Jurisprudence*, p. 361.

[30] *Kobez*, I, 26.

[30a] Ibid.

[31] The Itinerary of Pethachia M. E. Carmoly.

[32] On the RaBaD see L. Ginzberg, *JE* I.

[33] See *Luzatto, Kerem Hemed* III, p. 67. Ginzberg, ibid.

[34] See *Responsa*, ed. Freimann, p. 234.

[35] Ibid p. 235.

[36] The *Sefer Ha Mitzvot* was translated into Latin in the 13th century. In the *Tractatus de Erroribus Philosopherum*, the *Sefer ha Mitzvot* is quoted. It was translated into French by M. Bloch "*Le livre des Precepts par Moise ben Maimon*, Paris 1888. It was edited several times. Lately, it was edited by Ch. Heller. See M. Peritz, "Das Buch der Gesetze, *Moses ben Maimon*". II, p. 439. Also F. Rosenthal, ibid.

CHAPTER IX

[1] Munk, *Notice sur Joseph ben Jehouda*, p. 33.

[2] Graetz, (Hebrew V), p. 400.

[3] Bibl. *Arab. Hispanae*, p. 293. Munk, *Arch. Israelites*, 1861.

[4] Idem, *Joseph ben Jehouda*.

[5] Ibid. *Kobez*, II, 30; *Birchat Abraham*. ed. Goldberg. Comp. particularly, Asaf, *Tarbiz*, 1920-1930.

[6] See Asaf, ibid. 125-128; No. 2, p. 64 and 66.

[7] Ibid.; *Kobez*, ibid. *Birchat Abraham*.

[8] Kobez, *Birchat Abraham*; Munk, ibid.

[9] Ibid.

[10] Asaf, ibid.

[11] *Birchat Abraham*; Munk, ibid.

[12] In the year 1503 of the era of the Contracts.

[13] *M'amar, Tehiyat ha-Metim*, was written in Arabic and was translated into the Hebrew by Ibn Tibbon and Al-Harizi. See Steinschneider, *Hebræische Uebersetzungen*, p. 431.

[13a] See Aristotle, Politics, I, 3, "Nature makes nothing without purpose or in vain".

[14] Isaiah: XXVIII, 13.

[15] *Responsa*, ed. Freimann pp. 62, 71, and pp. 363, 367.

[16] *Kobez*, II, 15; *Responsa*, XIV.

[17] *Kobez*; ibid.; *Hemdah Genuzah*, pp. 3-6.

CHAPTER X

[1] The entire book was completed about 1195. See Marx, *H.U.C.A.* 1926.

[2] Comp. D. Kaufmann, *Die Geschichte der Attributenlehre*, 1877.

[3] See Robertson Smith, *The Religion of the Semites*, p. 311.

[4] According to Josephus, *Ant.* IV, 8, it was forbidden to wear garments made of linen and wool because the priest wore such garments.
[5] Comp. Josephus, ibid. Talmud, *Nazir.* 59a.
[6] According to the Talmud, Mak. 11a, the reason a man who unintentionally killed another must remain in exile until the death of the High Priest is because the latter did not pray for the welfare of his generation.
[7] Comp. *Mechilta,* XII. Also Ibn Ezra to Exodus. l.c.
[8] Comp. Aristotle, *Nic. Ethics* VIII, 9. "For it may be noticed that the sacrifices and festivals of ancient origin take place after harvest, being in fact harvest-festivals; this is because that was the season of the year at which people had most leisure".
[9] See Tacitus, *History* III, 24.
[10] *B.B.* 25a.
[11] *Midrash Rabba,* Lev. XIII, 5.
[12] See Robertson Smith, *The Religion of the Semites,* p. 215; 364.
[13] Comp. *Targum* Gen. XLIII, 22. "The animals which the Egyptians worshipped, the Hebrews ate."
[14] See Robertson Smith, 272.
[15] Philo is of the same opinion. Comp. his essay on *Circumcision,* Ed. Young, III, p. 175.
[16] See Josephus, *Contra Apion,* II, 13. Also Tacitus, *Hist.* V. 5.
[17] Sanh. 21b. Maimonides himself says in the *Mishne Torah* that some *Hukkim* cannot be explained rationally.
[18] More about *Hukkim* and *Halacha,* the reader will find in my forthcoming book, *The History and Development of the Halacha.*
[19] Comp. S. Eppenstein, "Beitrage zur Pentateuchexegese Maimunis", *Moses ben Maimon,* I, p. 411; Comp. also Yellin, *Tarbiz,* 1930, p. 93.
[20] See below chapter XV.
[20a] See Moreh II, 25.
[21] *Theologico-Political Treatise,* ch. VII.
[22] Ibid. Ch. VIII.
[23] Moreh, III, 34.
[24] Comp. his letter to Pinchas, the Dayyan of Alexandria, *Kobez* I, 26.
[25] See *Nid.* 61b. Comp. also *Tosefot,* l.c.
[26] See his introduction to the Moreh.
[27] *Birchat Abraham;* Munk, *Joseph ben Iehouda,* p. 26.
[28] Munk ibid. p. 27, note 1.
[29] It was called *Dux Neutrorum Sive Dubiorum.* This title is quoted by Albert the Great in his *Summa.* See P. Mandonnet *Siger de Brabant,* 1908.

CHAPTER XI

[1] Introduction to the Commentary on the Mishna.
[2] *Deot;* and *Lulov.*

[3] Sanhedrin, XXV, Maimonides as well as Plato believed that the government should be directed by men who are scholars.
[4] *Kobez,* I, 12. See *Responsa,* ed. Fr. p. 325.
[5] Ibid. p. 14.
[6] *Moreh,* III, 51.
[7] See *Cambridge Medieval Hist.* VI, p. 725.
[8] Shem Tov, Moreh. III, 51.
[9] *Deot.* Also see Commentary on *Abot,* 3-4.
[10] *Eight Chapters,* IV. Commentary on *Abot* 4.
[11] *Deot.*
[12] Ibid. Comp. Plato, *Laws,* VI, "The bride and bridegroom must set their minds to produce for the state, children". Comp. also *idem.* VIII.
[12a] See Commentary to the Mishna, Sanh. X.
[13] Responsa, p. 28; 40.
[14] Comp. Israel Davidson, *Thesaurus* I.
[15] *Eight Chapters,* V. Comp. also Aristotle, Politics, VIII.
[16] *Abadim* IX.
[17] Ibid. I.
[18] Commentary to *Abot* I.
[19] *Abadim* I.
[20] *Sechirut* XI.
[21] Ibid. XIII, Comp. *Tosefta,* B. M. VIII.
[22] *Sechirut X.* See B. M. 109.
[23] Moreh III, 27; 49. Comp Aristotle, *Nic. Ethics* IX, 9. "For a man is a social being and designed by nature to be with others".
[24] *Deot* VI.
[25] Ibid. V.
[26] *Moreh* III, 41.
[27] *Issure Biah* XI, Comp. also *Yebamot* 62b. See *Tosefot,* l.c.
[28] *Melachim* IV. *Gezelah we-Abedah* V.
[29] *Rozeah* II, 11 Comp. Aristotle *Nic. Eth.* V, 11. "It seems to be against the state rather than against himself; for he suffers voluntarily, and nobody suffers injustices voluntarily. This is why the state exacts a penalty; suicide is punished by certain marks of dishonour, as being an offence against the state." In Athens, a suicide's hand was buried apart from the body. According to Josephus, *Bell. Jud.* III, a suicide's body was to be exposed the whole day and buried only after sunset. This was a means of dishonor.
[30] *Matnat Anyym,* I-X.
[31] *Melachim,* VIII.
[32] *Responsa,* pp. 40-41.
[33] Ibid. p. 335.
[34] Commentary on the Mishna, *Ab. Zarah.*
[35] *Responsa,* p. 332.
[36] Ibid. 47. Mamrim III.

[37] *Akum* XI. See RaBaD l.c. See Ginzberg *J. E.* article RaBaD.
[38] *Mezuzah.*
[39] *Eight Chapters,* VIII. The letter on Astrology to the Jews of Provençal.
[40] See the Letter, ibid.
[41] *Tfilah* I.
[42] *Moreh* III, 51.
[43] *Tefilah* XI.
[44] *Responsa* p. 6.
[45] Ibid. 338; 328.
[46] *Kidush ha Hodesh* XVII.
[47] Ibid. *Moreh* II, 11; Josephus was also of the opinion that the Jews in ancient times wrote books on scientific subjects. *Contra Apion.*
[48] *Moreh* III, 27; 34.
[49] *Mamrim* II.
[50] Ibid.
[51] Ibid.
[52] Introduction to the commentary on the Mishna.
[53] *Moreh,* III, 40.
[54] Ibid, III, 17.
[55] Ibid. and 51.
[56] Ibid. II, 35-48. Also *Yesode ha-Torah.*
[57] *Moreh* II, 36.
[58] He finished chapter 40 as follows: "Note what is meant by these words."
[59] Commentary on the Mishna, Sanhedrin. See also, *Teshuba.*
[60] Josephus, *Bell. J.* VII, 7.
[61] *The Treatise on Resurrection.*
[62] Sanh. 90b.
[63] Commentary on the Mishna, Sanhedrin. See also Talmud, l.c.
[64] *Moreh* I, 42.
[65] *The Treatise on Resurrection.* Also Maimonides' Letter to Hashdai ha-Levi. *Kobez* II, 24.
[66] *Moreh* I, 70. Cf. Also *Yesode ha-Torah.*
[67] *Teshuba* VIII.
[68] See S. Zeitlin, *Josephus on Jesus.* p. 70.
[69] *Melachim* XI-XII; *Teshuba;* Commentary on the Mishna Sanhedrin.
[70] Ibid. Ch. 1.
[71] Sanhedrin XIV.
[72] *Melachim* VIII.

CHAPTER XII

[1] *Bibl. Arab. Hisp.* p. 293; Alkifti was a contemporary of Maimonides.
[2] "et Francorum Regis Ascaloniae ipsum (Maimonides) maxime optantis, Medicus electus est, quod tamen munus et honorem omnino recusavit. Ibid.

[3] Maimonides' letter to Samuel ibn Tibbon. Kobez II, 28.
[4] See Mann, "*The Jews in Egypt*", II, 316.
[5] *Responsa,* pp. 152-3.
[6] Ibid. pp. 32-37.
[7] Ibid. p. 82.
[8] Ibid. pp. 153-55.
[9] The slave claimed that she was a Jewess. *Responsa* p. 152.
[10] See A. Marx. *H. U. C. A.* 1926, pp. 311-358. *Kobez,* II, 24.
[11] "The Eleventh of Tishri 1507 to the era of the contracts". See ibid.
[12] *Responsa* III, LVIII; See Marx ibid; *Kobez,* ibid.
[12a] *Kobez,* I, 6.
[13] Weil, *Geshichte der Chalifen,* III, 432.
[14] Responsa LVIII-LXI. Also XLIV.
[15] *Kobez* I, 7-12.
[15a] Wertheimer, *Ginze Yerushalaim* 1846. *Ozar Nehmad,* II, 3.
[16] See Marx *H. U. C. A.* 1926. p. 331.
[17] Wertheimer, *Ginze Yerushalaim,* 1896.
[18] *Kobez,* II, 26.
[18a] Comp. *Ginze Yerushalaim,* p. 36.
[19] *Kobez,* II, 26.
[20] Ibid. 44, *Ozar Nehmad* II, 3. See Marx, ibid.
[21] *Kobez* II, 36-37; *Hemda Genuza,* 23-25.
[22] *Kobez* 23-24.

CHAPTER XIII

[1] Munk, *Notice sur Joseph ben Iehouda* p. 29-30.
[2] *Birchat Abraham,* ed. Goldberg. See also Carmoly *History of the Jewish Physicians,* Baltimore; A. Friedenwald, *Jewish Physicians,* Philadelphia; J. Pogel, "Maimuni als Medizinischer Schriftststeller, *Moses ben Maimon,* I, 231-249; See G. Sarton Introduction to the Hist. of Science, Baltimore, 1931; D. Campbell, Arabian Medicine, London, 1926. Eiger, *Yevreiskaya Mysl,* Leningrad, 1926.
[3] See Steinschneider, Arabishe Literatur, 158; See Pogel, ibid.
[4] Cf. also *Deot.*
[5] A Hebrew translation was published in *Kerem Hemed,* III; see Steinschneider, Hebraeischie Uebersetzungen, 770.
[6] Grossberg, *Sepher Rephuoth,* London 1900.
[7] Steinschneider, Arabishe Literatur, See 158, See Kroner, *Die Haemorrhoiden in der Medicin des XII und XIII Jahrhunderts.* Harlem, 1911.
[8] It was translated into Hebrew by Moses ibn Tibbon. See Steinschneider, *Gifte und ihre Heilung von Moses Maimonides,* Berlin, 1873. See also Steinschneider, *Jeshurun,* Kabak, 1864.
[9] H. Kroner, *Geschichte der Medizin des XII. Jahrhunderts,* 1906. It was dedicated to the Sultan of Hamat, who was the nephew of Saladin.
[10] See H. Adler, *Miscellany of Hebrew Literature,* Vol. I, London.

CHAPTER XIV

[1] See the Introduction to *Zedah Laderech*, by Menachem ben Zerah; also *Sefer ha-Kabbalah.*
[2] Comp. Maimonides' Letter to Joseph ibn Aknin, *Birchat Abraham.*
[3] Maimonides' Letter to Ibn Gabir; *Kobez* II, 16; also the Letter to Ibn Aknin; Ibid. 30.
[4] Ibid. I, 27.
[5] Ibid. II, 29.
[6] Ibid. 31.
[7] The letter to Hasdai, Ibid. 24.
[8] Ibid. 44. Responsa, Lx.
[9] *Sefer Yuhasin*, ed. Filopowsky, 1857, p. 220.
[10] Ibid.

CHAPTER XV

[1] Born about 1180.
[2] *Kobez.* III, 11.
[3] See A. Marx, *JQR.* 1935. Dr. Marx was kind enough to let me have the manuscript before it was given for publication.
[4] Meir Abulafia was the author of some important treatise on Halacha. Meir answered his opponent, in which he defended his views. The letters were collected and added by Brill *Kitab al Rassia*—(a treatise of letters) Paris, 1871.
[5] *Kobez,* III, 16.
[6] Ibid. 16.
[7] See the letter of Solomon of Montpellier, *Jeshurun,* VIII.
[8] Comp. *Kobez,* III, 18.
[9] Ibid. 16-17.
[10] Ibid. 6, The *Mishne Torah* is here referred to as the *Yad ha- Hazakah* for the first time and since so called. Comp. *Kobez* III, 21.
[11] Ibid. 6.
[12] Ibid. 4.
[13] Ibid. 1.
[14] Ibid. 4. About the sequence of the letters, see Graetz, (Hebrew) V. p. 349. See, Geiger, *Ozar Nehmad,* 17, pp. 170-171.
[15] *Kobez* III; See Graetz, V, p. 45.
[16] *Kobez.* Ibid.
[17] *Jeshurun* VIII, 98. See note 1.
[18] *Kobez* III, 8.
[19] Comp. also *Cambridge Medieval History,* V. p. 818.
[20] Comp. the letter of Hillel of Verona; *Kobez,* III, 13. Also the letter of Judah and Abraham the sons of Hasdai, *Jeshurun,* VIII, 53.
[21] *Kobez,* III, 4.
[22] Ibid.
[23] *Jeshurun* VIII pp. 89-94.

[24] Ibid. pp. 21-47.
[25] Ibid. 125-155. Also *Ozar Nehmad*, II, 170.
[26] See Ibid. *Jeshurun* VIII, 48-56. Comp. also N. Brüll, Die Polemik fur und Gegen, Maimuni im Dreizehnten Jahrhunderte, *Jahrbücher fur Iüdische Geschichte*, 1879.
[27] *Kobez*, III, 21.
[28] *Cambridge Medieval History*, VI, 717.
[29] See the letter of Hillel; *Kobez*, III, 14. Cf. Jeshurun, p. 51.
[30] Cf. The letter of Hillel; *Kobez* III, 14. See also Graetz V, 63.
[31] The letter of Hillel, Kobez III, 14.
[32] The Introduction to *Magen Abot.*
[33] P. Mandonnet, "*Siger de Brabant et L'Averroisme Latin au XIII Siecle,* Part I, Louvain 1911. See also E. Renan, *Averroes et L'Averroisme,* Paris.
[34] *Kobez*, III, 21-24. *Jeshurun*, 7.
[35] Ibid. 14.
[36] See Responsa of Solomon ibn Adret ed. Venice, 1545, p. 65-75. Also *Minhat Kanaot*, Pressburg; also *Igrot Ha-Rashboah*, Warsaw 1888; Graetz, (Hebrew) V, 217. This ban was limited only to fifty years.
[37] *Kerem Hemed* III, 67, However, the verdict of the people is against the opinion of Luzzatto. Maimonides was called *RaM b'MaZaL-* i.e. Rabbi Moses, the son of Maimon, the fortunate one for his books were studied. The RaBaD was called RaBAD- Rabbi Abraham, (Abad) the lost one since his books were not studied and were lost. Comp. Sambari. M. J. C. I, 124.
[38] *Kerem Hemed* IV,
[39] Ahad Ha-Am, "*Essay on Zionism*" p. 211, London 1922.
[40] *Ha-Shahar*, 1875. pp. 131-134.

CHAPTER XVI

[1] Munk, *Notice sur Joseph ben Iehouda*, p. 27,
[2] "Et illa quorum utilitas scitur, vocat Rabi Moyses Judaeus judicia alia vocat ceremonalia generali nomine." Comp. *Moreh*, III, 26.
[3] See Joel, *Verhaltnis Alberts des Grossen zu Maimonides*, Breslau 1863.
[4] "Praeterea Rabbi Moyses dicit, quod Deus est ens non in essentia et vivens non in vita et potens non in potentia et sapiens non in sapientia. Ergo in Deo non est aliud essentia quam esse." *Quaest. disput.* Comp. *Moreh* 1; also "Praeterea Rabbi Moyses dicit, quod hujusmodi nomina non significant in Deo intentiones additas supra ejus essentiam. Omne enim accidens significat intentionem additam supra essentiam sui subjecti; ergo praedicta nomina non significant accidens in Deo." Comp. *Moreh*, Ibid. See Guttmann, Der Einfluss der maimonidischen Philosophie aus das christliche Abendland. *Moses ben Maimon*, p. 135-230.
[5] In a letter to Isak Casaubonus Scaliger expressed great admiration

for the *Moreh Nebuchim. Epistolae Josephin Scalligeri,* Lugduni Batavorum, 1677.

[6] Comp. Louis-Germain Levy *Maimonide,* Paris, p. 271. Also D. Kaufmann, Der Führer Maimuni's in der Weltliteratur, Gesammelte Schriften, II, 1910.

[7] See H. Wolfson, *The Philosophy of Spinoza,* Cambridge, 1934. "Now, the religion of reason which Spinoza briefly outlines for us here is nothing but a modified form of the philosophic conception of Judaism as described by Maimonides." X. II, 328 passim.

[8] "My reverence for this great teacher went so far, that I regarded him as the ideal of a perfect man, and looked upon his teachings as if they had been inspired with Divine Wisdom itself. . . . I swear, by the reverence which I owe my great teacher, Rabbi Moses ben Maimon." J. Clark Murray, *Solomon Maimon,* p. xiv.

[9] His Introduction to *Semag.*

[10] Comp. Ibn Ezra, Commentary to Deut. 1, 2.

[11] Emden, *Mitpachat Sefarim.*

[12] See his commentary on the *Mishne Torah, Yesode ha-Torah.* The letter to Ibn Aknin which is known as Megillat Setarim was compiled by one of the Kabbalists and attributed to Maimonides. Similarly the "Treatise on External Bliss," the "Will to His Son," and the "Oath and Prayer" were not written by Maimonides.

[13] See Graetz, (Hebrew) VII, p. 215.

[14] *Zedah la-Derch,* Maamar II, 4. passim.

[15] *Sefer beth ha-behira,* to Nedarim.

[16] Comp. Solomon Luria, Introduction to *Yam Shelomo,* Hullin.

[17] *Yad Malachi* and others.

INDEX